REGIONAL COOPERATION AND INTEGRATION IN ASIA AND THE PACIFIC

RESPONDING TO THE COVID-19 PANDEMIC AND "BUILDING BACK BETTER"

JANUARY 2022

ADB

IsDB البنك الإسلامي للتنمية
Islamic Development Bank

CONTENTS

CASE STUDY, TABLES, FIGURES, AND BOXES

FOREWORD

In 2020, the world united to combat the coronavirus disease (COVID-19) pandemic. Global and regional cooperation on public health has been unprecedented. Progress in economic integration, however, has been mixed. While pre-pandemic arguments against globalization, along with some renewed protectionism, continue to pose major risks to a post–COVID-19 recovery, economies in Asia and the Pacific have continued entering megaregional and interregional trade and investment agreements. In addition, countries are working toward meeting their nationally determined contributions under the landmark 2015 United Nations Climate Change Conference. The crisis offers a unique opportunity to move cooperation forward.

The pandemic has three main impacts on global and regional development. One, it tragically continues to cause significant loss of life. Two, it slowed and, in some cases, unraveled development gains, exposing vulnerabilities that had grown alongside or because of those gains. And three, the pandemic is accelerating positive trends that are transforming the world, such as the digitalization of public services, flexible and remote work, paperless trade, and other innovations.

Regional cooperation and integration (RCI) in Asia and the Pacific is led and owned by countries and conducted mainly within and between subregions. Multilateral development banks (MDBs) assist countries individually and collectively, mobilizing their own considerable and varied resources to help developing countries expedite their collective decisions through jointly agreed programs and projects that deliver cross-border benefits. The pandemic was an extraordinary wake-up call to the international development community to expand, intensify, and build new cross-border development partnerships among countries and with MDBs.

The Asian Development Bank, Asian Infrastructure Investment Bank, European Bank for Reconstruction and Development, Islamic Development Bank, and World Bank Group came together as the major MDBs operating in the Asia and Pacific region to take stock of efforts to help countries in the region confront the pandemic, reflect on progress and lessons learned, and deliberate on strategic directions for national and RCI efforts. This report is the product of our recent collaboration, and we encourage all RCI stakeholders to examine its findings and consider their potential application.

Finally, we express our appreciation to all country and MDB contributors who made the report possible. We are especially grateful to the Asian Development Bank for serving as secretariat.

Bambang Susantono
Vice-President
Asian Development Bank

Joachim von Amsberg
Special Advisor to the President
Asian Infrastructure Investment Bank

Beata Javorcik
Chief Economist
European Bank for Reconstruction and Development

Amer Bukvic
Acting Director General, Global Practice and Partnership
Islamic Development Bank

Hartwig Schafer
Vice-President
World Bank Group

ACKNOWLEDGMENTS

This report was jointly prepared by the Asian Development Bank (ADB), the Asian Infrastructure Investment Bank (AIIB), the European Bank for Reconstruction and Development (EBRD), the Islamic Development Bank (IsDB), and the World Bank Group. ADB is the lead publisher of this report and its publication guidelines apply.

The report's preparation was led by Hung Ba Nguyen, senior regional cooperation specialist, ADB; Jang Ping Thia, lead economist and manager, Economics Department, AIIB; Alexander Plekhanov, director, Transition Impact and Global Economics, EBRD; Riad Ragueb, acting director, Regional Cooperation and Integration Department, IsDB; and Mandakini Kaul, senior regional cooperation offi cer, South Asia Regional Integration and Engagement, World Bank.

The contributing authors are as follows: ADB consultants Christopher MacCormac, with support from Peter Fedon, the overview, Chapter 2 and conclusion; Jang Ping Thia, AIIB, Chapter 3; Zsoka Koczan, senior economist, and Philipp Paetzold, analyst, EBRD, Chapter 4; Kadir Basboga, senior regional integration and trade economist, with support from Imed Drine, lead economist; Nazar Diab, senior market integration specialist; Afrah Khalifa, project coordinator, IsDB, Chapter 5; and Muthukumara Mani, lead economist, World Bank, Chapter 6.

The authors are grateful for inputs from speakers at the webinar series representing governments, international organizations, and other stakeholders, as well as from members of the ADB Regional Cooperation and Integration (RCI) Committee, led by Xiaoqin (Emma) Fan, director, Public Management, Financial Sector, and Regional Cooperation Division, East Asia Department; Safdar Parvez, advisor, East Asia Department; Thiam Hee (Bernard) Ng, director, Regional Cooperation and Operations Coordination Division, South Asia Department; Alfredo Perdiguero, director, Regional Cooperation and Operations Coordination Division, Southeast Asia Department; Cyn-Young Park, director, Regional Cooperation and Integration Division, Economic Research and Regional Cooperation Department; Rosalind McKenzie, principal operations coordination specialist, Pacifi c Department; and (John) Juhyun Jeong, investment specialist, Private Sector Operation Department.

The ADB RCI-TG team under the guidance of Ronald Butiong, chief of the RCI Thematic Group, coordinated overall production, with support from Yuebin Zhang, principal regional cooperation specialist; Wilhelmina Paz, economist (regional cooperation); Melanie Pre, operations analyst; and Rosalie Aboleda, senior operations assistant.

Muriel Ordoñez copyedited the manuscript. Josef Ilumin created the cover design. Edith Creus did the layout and typesetting. Lawrence Casiraya proofread the material. The Printing Services Unit of ADB's Offi ce of Administrative Services and the publishing team of the Department of Communications supported the report's printing and publishing.

EXECUTIVE SUMMARY

The coronavirus disease (COVID-19) pandemic was of such unprecedented scale that only region-wide solidarity could beat it back, start to undo the cross-border economic damage wrought by measures to prevent the spread of the disease, and lay the basis for building back better. To stop cross-border contagion early in the pandemic, many countries closed their borders, severely reducing economic production and disrupting trade. They and their multilateral development bank (MDB) partners quickly understood that the pandemic could not be managed without intercountry cooperation.

Multilateral development banks and regional cooperation and integration. Five leading MDBs—the Asian Development Bank (ADB), the Asian Infrastructure Investment Bank (AIIB), the European Bank for Reconstruction and Development (EBRD), the Islamic Development Bank (IsDB), and the World Bank Group—used regional cooperation and integration (RCI) to tackle the pandemic and its aftermath among their members in Asia and the Pacific. The MDBs collaborated on a report to summarize the lessons they and their members have learned from the journey to recovery. The report is useful for anyone engaged in RCI.

In response to the pandemic, countries and areas quickly rallied through RCI platforms.[1] They maintained health services and tracked and controlled infection, kept essential goods flowing across borders, protected their people's welfare, and ensured fiscal stability. Transitioning from emergency measures, the subregions harnessed digital technologies to strengthen public health and harmonize trade procedures. Countries rolled out vaccines to keep their populations safe and reopen their borders. RCI encompasses various dimensions of sustainable and inclusive development: (i) promoting trade and investment, (ii) building connectivity infrastructure, (iii) improving people's mobility, (iv) strengthening provision of regional public goods, and (v) supporting the institutional basis for cross-border policy cooperation.

MDBs are helping countries cooperate by offering them bilateral and regional support. MDBs perform one or more roles: (i) convener or "honest broker," providing impartial information, advisory, logistics, and coordination services; (ii) capacity developer, strengthening national institutions and organizations to plan and implement RCI activities; (iii) knowledge broker,

---

[1] The Central Asia Regional Economic Cooperation (CAREC) Program (Afghanistan, Azerbaijan, the People's Republic of China [PRC], Georgia, Kazakhstan, the Kyrgyz Republic, Mongolia, Pakistan, Tajikistan, Turkmenistan, and Uzbekistan); the Greater Mekong Subregion (GMS) Program (Cambodia; Yunnan Province and Guangxi Zhuang Autonomous Region, PRC; the Lao People's Democratic Republic; Myanmar; Thailand; and Viet Nam); the South Asia Subregional Economic Cooperation (SASEC) Program (Bangladesh, Bhutan, India, Maldives, Myanmar, Nepal, and Sri Lanka); and the Pacific Islands Forum (PIF) (Australia, Cook Islands, the Federated States of Micronesia, Fiji, French Polynesia, Kiribati, Nauru, New Caledonia, New Zealand, Niue, Palau, Papua New Guinea, the Republic of Marshall Islands, Samoa, Solomon Islands, Tonga, Tuvalu, and Vanuatu). PIF leaders established the Council of Regional Organisations of the Pacific (CROP), to improve cooperation, coordination, and collaboration among the intergovernmental regional organizations to achieve sustainable development in the Pacific. ADB placed on hold its assistance in Afghanistan effective 15 August 2021. https://www.adb.org/news/adb-statement-afghanistan.

undertaking specialized sector, thematic, economic policy research, and other strategic studies from a cross-border perspective; (iv) technical advisor, helping plan, design, and implement RCI and cross-border collective action project and program interventions; and (v) financier, mobilizing resources to support the other four roles and to finance RCI projects and programs in priority sectors and thematic areas.

With MDBs' assistance, countries coordinated actions and shared knowledge and lessons, perhaps the most important of which is that countries and MDBs must pursue and deepen innovation to protect regional public health and prevent economic and social loss.

How to build back better. Countries and MDBs must continue to work together to ensure resilient trade and connectivity; quality infrastructure that will promote global value chains; and information and communication technology (ICT) that is within reach of most people and small firms, not just the well-educated and big business. MDBs must continue to help the region ensure the wider distribution of post-pandemic economic benefits, and help policy makers ensure that trade, investment, and migration reduce poverty and inequality within and between countries.

To build back better, the region must cooperate to quickly regain pre-pandemic levels of trade and industry. MDBs must continue to encourage greener infrastructure, logistics, and tourism; energy efficiency; and greater cross-border trade in renewable energy. Regional public goods such as air quality management must be a regional project because air pollution is not confined within national borders.

From crisis to opportunity. The tragic loss of life from the pandemic has been well documented, as has the severe reversal of socioeconomic development gains and the exposure of existing vulnerabilities that had developed alongside or because of those gains. But the pandemic has also accelerated the digitalization of public services and remote work, already ongoing before the pandemic, while fostering opportunities for innovation, such as paperless trade.

Although global, regional, and subregional cooperation to tackle COVID-19 has been extraordinary, pre-pandemic anti-globalization and protectionist trade sentiments continue to stifle post–COVID-19 recovery. Yet, the region's economies increasingly participate in megaregional and interregional multilateral trade and investment agreements. And they continue to hold to their nationally determined contributions under the 2015 COP21 agreement on climate change. This challenging time offers the chance to surpass the pre-pandemic situation.

The region's development partners, including MDBs, have contributed significantly to ending the emergency and starting the recovery. However, further innovations in knowledge work, technical and advisory services, programming of operations, and resource mobilization and allocation will be essential. The MDBs take varied and complementary approaches to the following themes and suggest how countries can collaborate and what trends they should consider to further the benefits of RCI, including stronger partnership with the MDBs:

Innovation and strengthening of collective action. Economies in Asia and the Pacific have long cooperated on a subregional and inter-subregional basis. They have taken interdisciplinary and multisector approaches to *regional public goods* (including regional health security); *greater connectivity; and trade, investment, and mobility*. With MDBs' assistance, economies have adopted new digital technologies and harmonized procedures and practices to expand trade; strengthened regional public health; increased South–South learning and technology sharing; and contributed to making tourism safer, more inclusive, and greener.

Quality regional connectivity. Connectivity is essential for regional and global trade, integration of national and cross-border infrastructure, expansion of the use of digital technologies, and net zero transition. Quality connectivity infrastructure, not low-cost labor, will determine how much future foreign direct investment will come in and where it will flow.

Inclusive trade, investment, and migration. Post–COVID-19 economic integration must reduce or at least mitigate economic inequality. MDBs must help policy makers ensure that trade, investment, and migration become more inclusive by strengthening social safety nets, education, and training; investing in infrastructure and logistics to encourage private investment; linking foreign-sponsored production facilities and local suppliers; and aligning trade and foreign investment with countries' skill base.

Regional approaches to manage air pollution in South Asia. Coordination in improving regional public goods, such as tackling transboundary issues of air pollution, is often the most effective and sustainable solution. Sources of air pollution are highly diverse in South Asia but air pollution management has been limited, focused on cities or municipal regions. The proposed "airshed approach," however, is a more useful concept for regional coordination in managing air pollution. Projections show that regionally coordinated measures with shared targets could provide the most cost-effective outcomes. Regional cooperation, therefore, is essential to promote regional public goods such as management of air pollution because of its cross-border nature.

Multilateral development banks as key partners in promoting regional cooperation and integration. Economic resilience requires cooperation and the global consequences of the COVID-19 crisis require interregional cooperation. MDBs are able to foster multistakeholder cooperation that can meet cross-border challenges. IsDB's innovative reverse linkage mechanism, for example, fosters peer-to-peer cooperation to design innovative development solutions. Innovative financing instruments, including Islamic finance schemes, can combine philanthropy, profit and loss sharing, and revenue-generating financing to expand access to financial services and promote socially responsible investment.

We believe the report will be useful to RCI practitioners across Asia and the Pacific. It shows how countries, assisted by MDBs, quickly widened and deepened RCI to face an existential threat. While the region was no stranger to cross-border health challenges, the COVID-19 pandemic was so perilous that it demanded intercountry coordination and collaboration and MDB assistance on regional health security at a scale and intensity not seen before. Countries led efforts to combat the pandemic and, with MDB assistance, helped avert what could have been a greater catastrophe.

We urge the reader to consider the nature and degree of RCI innovation being attempted. The medium- to longer-term perspective of some chapters has generated thought-provoking, research-based results to guide the formulation of country, regional, and interregional

RCI policies and strategies for inclusive and sustainable recovery. Regional policy makers, sector and thematic planners, and MDB officials will likely find them timely and valuable.

The report points to the indispensable role and the efficacy of the established RCI subregional programs and regional cooperation organizations such as the Pacific Community. They are the result of countries' own efforts and the essential and sustained support of MDBs. The pragmatic, flexible, consensus-based, and operations-focused nature and practices of the RCI architecture enabled countries and MDBs to act decisively against the pandemic. Those same characteristics will help support an RCI-based recovery.

That said, the report also points to a growing need for the RCI architecture to encompass a greater degree of inter-subregional cooperation, congruent with the expanding spatial impacts of challenges and opportunities of climate change and digital trade, among other regional public goods. RCI practitioners must find ways to retain the strong sense of subregional solidarity that exists in the established RCI platforms while enabling the RCI architecture to meet head on enormous region-wide challenges.

Precautions against the pandemic. A newspaper subeditor wears a face mask and gloves at his office in Dhaka, Bangladesh (photo by Abir Abdullah/ADB).

ABBREVIATIONS

ADB	Asian Development Bank
AIIB	Asian Infrastructure Investment Bank
AQM	air quality management
ASEAN	Association of Southeast Asian Nations
CAREC	Central Asia Regional Economic Cooperation
CCS	carbon capture and storage
COVID-19	coronavirus disease
CROP	Council of Regional Organisations of the Pacific
DMC	developing member country
EBRD	European Bank for Reconstruction and Development
FDI	foreign direct investment
GAINS	Greenhouse Gas–Air Pollution Interactions and Synergies
GDP	gross domestic product
GHG	greenhouse gas
GMS	Greater Mekong Subregion
GVC	global value chain
ICT	information and communication technology
IsDB	Islamic Development Bank
MDB	multilateral development bank
OECD	Organisation for Economic Co-operation and Development
PIF	Pacific Islands Forum
$PM_{2.5}$	particulate matter
PRC	People's Republic of China
RCEP	Regional Comprehensive Economic Partnership
RCI	regional cooperation and integration
RCO	regional cooperation organization
SARS	severe acute respiratory syndrome
SASEC	South Asia Subregional Economic Cooperation
SMEs	small and medium-sized enterprises
WHO	World Health Organization
WTO	World Trade Organization

1 Overview

Introduction

Multilateral development banks (MDBs) are leading institutions through which the international development community channels finance, expertise, and knowledge to advance the socioeconomic and environmental development of countries and regions. MDBs were founded at different times, with unique memberships, charters and legal identities, organization structures, and access to resources, and almost all are headquartered at different locations. But MDBs have developed operational partnerships; engaged in operational cofinancing and knowledge sharing; coordinated on sector, country, subregional, and global development policy; and worked together in direct and/or complementary ways to respond to crises and deal with their aftermath.

The Asia and Pacific region's experience with the unfolding coronavirus disease (COVID-19) pandemic has highlighted the importance of regional cooperation and integration (RCI), emphasizing intercountry coordination and common approaches among countries to guide and leverage national efforts to combat the disease and to plan and start recovery for mutual benefit. Since the onset of the pandemic, the region has ramped up cooperation to secure public health and sustain trade flows amid severe disruption. In the absence of cross-border coordination, countries would be hard put to plan for reciprocal and mutually safe methods for lifting lockdowns and border restrictions; more resilient long-distance supply chains; reduction of risks of disease transmission from cross-border trade and mobility of people; cross-border accreditation of skills to strengthen the competitiveness of regional businesses; and the unique needs of migrant workers, landlocked countries, and countries that are fragile or in a post-conflict situation.

The report is the product of collaboration among five of the leading MDBs, each aiding its developing member countries in the Asia and Pacific region: the Asian Development Bank (ADB), the Asian Infrastructure Investment Bank (AIIB), the European Bank for Reconstruction and Development (EBRD), the Islamic Development Bank (IsDB), and the World Bank Group. The report discusses how they used RCI to assist countries during the emergency phase of the COVID-19 pandemic and how MDBs may play a continuing but evolving role during the region's transition to recovery and "build back better" a more inclusive and sustainable future.

Regional cooperation and integration is a key component of development policies and assistance, encompassing various dimensions of sustainable and inclusive development: promoting trade and investment, building connectivity infrastructure, improving people's mobility, strengthening provision of regional public goods, and supporting the institutional basis for cross-border policy cooperation.

The next part of this chapter presents an overview of RCI, the role of MDBs in RCI, and the main findings of the five ensuing chapters, each authored by an MDB and covering an RCI theme: (i) innovation and strengthening of collective action (Chapter 2, ADB); (ii) quality regional connectivity (Chapter 3, AIIB); (iii) inclusive trade, investment, and migration (Chapter 4, EBRD); (iv) regional approaches to support air pollution management in South Asia (Chapter 5, the World Bank); and (v) MDBs as key partners in promoting RCI (Chapter 6, IsDB).

The closing chapter summarizes how RCI stakeholders can use the information and findings of the report to widen, deepen, and evolve RCI so that it plays a more strategic and integral role in the development of Asia and the Pacific.

Importance, Nature, and Architecture of Regional Cooperation and Integration in Asia and the Pacific

Development and development assistance across the Asia and Pacific region take two approaches: one focused on countries and the other driven by regional and global issues, with a substantial share of development resources channeled through regional programs and activities. Individual countries and their development partners, including several major MDBs,[1] design and implement development programs and projects that keep both approaches in balance and strive to realize complementarities and even integration among them. This balance calls for strategic operational partnership among countries and MDBs to take on a range of development challenges effectively.

---

[1]   ADB, AIIB, EBRD, IsDB, and the World Bank Group.

Fighting the pandemic. Workers at the Beijing Naton Technology Group assembly line produce medical masks (photo by Deng Jia/ADB).

RCI is a key component of development assistance, encompassing various dimensions of sustainable and inclusive development: promoting trade and investment, building connectivity infrastructure, improving people's mobility, strengthening provision of regional public goods, and supporting the institutional basis for cross-border policy cooperation. Historical trends in the Asia and Pacific region show that RCI—evidenced by international movements of goods, capital, and people—has a significant and positive effect on economic growth and helps reduce poverty, although at varying degrees across the regions. Trade and investment, money and finance, and institutional and social interactions contribute to poverty reduction, particularly in lower-income countries. The overall extent of regional integration appears to influence poverty reduction more than efforts to promote individual approaches to regional integration (ADB 2018).

RCI in Asia and the Pacific is mainly—but not exclusively—subregional.[2] Effective and impactful RCI relies first and foremost on the continued ownership and leadership of the country groupings and the alignment with and adding of value to national development plans. Collective leadership provided by direct cooperation among senior officials supplies the framework for subregions to act jointly in response to emerging development opportunities and at times powerful challenges, such as the COVID-19 pandemic. While agreeing on positive long-term visions for mutually beneficial development under various subregional frameworks (Table 1), countries cooperate on planning and implementing sector and thematic programs and projects to pursue well-defined medium-term goals. Countries have established other subregional platforms where they discuss policy and build confidence in their own ability to promote RCI, with support from various development partners.

Table 1: Regional Cooperation and Integration Subregional Programs and the Pacific Community—High-Level Strategic Directions and Priorities

CAREC	GMS	SASEC	Pacific Community
CAREC 2030 Strategic Framework	**GMS 2030**	**SASEC: Powering Asia in the 21st Century**	**Framework for Pacific Regionalism**
"Connecting the region for shared and sustainable development" • Economic and financial stability • Trade, tourism, and economic corridors • Infrastructure and economic connectivity • Agriculture and water • Human development	"To develop a more integrated, prosperous, sustainable and equitable subregion" **Strengths** • Connectivity • Competitiveness • Community **Principles** • Environmental sustainability and resilience • Internal and external integration • Inclusivity	"Generate synergies through regional cooperation and enhanced integration to unleash latent potential" • Economic diversification • Accelerated economic growth • Inclusive and sustainable growth • Positive externalities and reduced poverty • Energy access and security	"Our Pacific vision is for a region of peace, harmony, security, social inclusion and prosperity, so that all Pacific people can lead free, healthy and productive lives." Effective and innovative application of science and knowledge in 20 sectors, guided by a deep understanding of Pacific Island contexts and cultures

CAREC = Central Asia Regional Economic Cooperation, GMS = Greater Mekong Subregion, SASEC = South Asia Subregional Economic Cooperation.
Source: Asian Development Bank.

---

[2]   The main RCI subregional entities include the Central Asia Regional Economic Cooperation (CAREC) Program (Afghanistan, Azerbaijan, the People's Republic of China [PRC], Georgia, Kazakhstan, the Kyrgyz Republic, Mongolia, Pakistan, Tajikistan, Turkmenistan, and Uzbekistan); the Greater Mekong Subregion (GMS) Program (Cambodia; Yunnan Province and Guangxi Zhuang Autonomous Region, PRC; the Lao People's Democratic Republic; Myanmar; Thailand; and Viet Nam); the South Asia Subregional Economic Cooperation (SASEC) Program (Bangladesh, Bhutan, India, Maldives, Myanmar, Nepal, and Sri Lanka); and the Pacific Islands Forum (PIF) (Australia, Cook Islands, the Federated States of Micronesia, Fiji, French Polynesia, Kiribati, Nauru, New Caledonia, New Zealand, Niue, Palau, Papua New Guinea, the Republic of Marshall Islands, Samoa, Solomon Islands, Tonga, Tuvalu, and Vanuatu). PIF leaders established the Council of Regional Organisations of the Pacific (CROP), to improve cooperation, coordination, and collaboration among the intergovernmental regional organizations to achieve sustainable development in the Pacific. ADB placed on hold its assistance in Afghanistan effective 15 August 2021. https://www.adb.org/news/adb-statement-afghanistan.

Multilateral Development Banks as Valuable Partners for Regional Cooperation and Integration

MDBs play several important roles in supporting regional and subregional initiatives in Asia and the Pacific. While an MDB's engagement and relationships across individual subregional cooperation entities may vary,[3] MDBs generally act as one or more of the following: (i) convener, with secretariat functions, an "honest broker," providing impartial information, advisory, logistics, and coordination services at various operational and administrative levels; (ii) capacity developer, enabling national institutions and organizations to plan and implement RCI activities; (iii) knowledge broker, undertaking specialized sector and thematic and economic policy research and other strategic studies from a cross-border perspective; (iv) technical advisor, helping plan, design, and implement RCI and cross-border collective action project and program interventions; and (v) financier, mobilizing resources to support the other four roles and to finance RCI projects and programs in priority sectors and thematic areas. The roles are mutually supportive and reinforcing, enabling MDBs to expedite, support, and promote RCI holistically and strategically. With their country and regional presence and deep technical expertise, MDBs help cohere regional issues and programs with country implementation, foster dialogue among countries across subregions, and further harmonize among themselves and other development finance partners aid efforts in support of cross-border cooperation.

Regional Cooperation and Integration and COVID-19

The Asia and Pacific region is no stranger to responding to crises with RCI. The Asian financial crisis of 1997 resulted in the establishment of the Chiang Mai Initiative. The first regional currency swap arrangement, it was launched by the Association of Southeast Asian Nations (ASEAN)+3 at an ADB meeting in May 2000 to resolve short-term liquidity difficulties and to supplement existing international financial arrangements. Over the past 2 decades, the region's countries, with support from MDBs and other partners, have implemented projects that thwarted sudden and serious outbreaks of national and cross-border spread of communicable and infectious diseases (e.g., severe acute respiratory syndrome [SARS], avian flu, HIV/AIDS, tuberculosis), strengthening regional health security (see Chapter 2).

The COVID-19 pandemic spread rapidly across Asia and the Pacific, and some countries' initial responses adversely impacted national economic activity and cross-border flows. To mitigate cross-border contagion, many countries shuttered their borders and constrained international movement of people (ADB 2020). Local and cross-border control measures severely reduced economic production and disrupted supplies and cross-border trade (Figure 1). The initial emergency phase and subsequent waves of new COVID-19 variants have "left no country behind," harming the quality of life of every MDB developing member country in Asia and the Pacific. Countries and their MDB partners quickly grasped that the pandemic was an unprecedented global and regional development challenge that could not be managed in either the near or longer term without substantial and sustained intercountry cooperation.

---

[3]   ADB has the lead responsibility for providing vital secretariat services of CAREC, GMS, and SASEC. ADB works closely and regularly with national coordinators in that capacity in providing technical, administrative, and coordinating support to the ministerial meetings and sector forums and working groups.

Figure 1: Regional Cooperation and Integration–Related Impacts of COVID-19 in Asia and the Pacific, 2020

50%
decline in region exports

Trade fell, then rebounded.
- Border closures, lockdowns, quarantines, and other means to control the virus spread disrupted the region's supply chains.
- Intraregional trade within Asia declines during the first half of 2020. Yet, increased demand for goods related to the COVID-19 pandemic and electronics drove a rebound in developing Asia's exports.

0%
international tourist arrivals between Jan and Apr 2020

Tourism imploded; remittances were broadly steady.
- Tourism collapsed in all economies.
- Remittances declined in many economies as border closures halted market-based labor migration, yet remittances increased in several other countries.

45%
dropped in intraregional greenfield investment for Jan–Aug 2020*

Significant declines in investment.
- The COVID-19 pandemic accentuated the prevailing downward trend in greenfield FDI inflows to the region.
* compared to the same period in 2019

Source: Asian Development Bank.

The cross-border effects of the pandemic emergency were felt in addition to ongoing pre-pandemic longer-term trends, which saw slowing of growth of trade and investment and rising protectionism among major international trading partners. The harsh efforts to control the pandemic, and sluggish global trade and investment were amplified by preexisting economic, social, and environmental vulnerabilities, such as income and gender inequality and climate change–related disasters triggered by natural hazards, among others. The combination of the various adverse impacts risked widening and deepening the already imbalanced progress on the Sustainable Development Goals (SDGs) within and between countries. Countries and their development partners, including MDBs, needed to collectively plan and manage the transition from emergency to recovery, based on closer and more sustained regional cooperation. They needed to consider how not only preexisting trends and vulnerabilities but also COVID-19–induced behavioral trends and expectations were generating new demands and prospects. The pandemic was accelerating the need for and adoption of cross-border e-commerce as well as e-government services in education, health care, environmental management, and banking and finance, plus more accessible and reliable information and communication technology platforms for digital trade and cross-border finance. Diverse and concerted collective action was required to plan and design policies, programs, and projects to "build back better" recovery that would leave no one and no country behind and reignite stalled progress on the SDGs (ADB, UNDP, and UNESCAP 2021).

The Joint Multilateral Development Bank Report

This report was not designed or intended to evaluate RCI in the context of COVID-19. Instead, it takes stock of the MDBs' efforts to help countries tackle the pandemic, reflects on the progress and lessons learned, and identifies the strategic directions for future and complementary national and RCI efforts in the region. We may use the findings of the five chapters that follow as knowledge and learning resources to appreciate the significance and efficacy of RCI in overcoming crises and achieving recovery. We believe the findings can help the two principal RCI actors—countries and MDBs—widen and deepen the scope of RCI and its benefits while opening up participation in RCI to more diverse stakeholders and partners.

Chapters on Regional Cooperation and Integration Themes

The report is organized around themes, the ways countries can collaborate effectively, and the key trends they should consider to expand the benefits of RCI, including through stronger partnership with the MDBs. The thematic chapters will discuss (i) innovation and strengthening of collective action (Chapter 2); (ii) quality regional connectivity (Chapter 3); (iii) inclusive trade, investment, and migration (Chapter 4); (iv) regional approaches to support air pollution management in South Asia (Chapter 5); and (v) MDBs as key partners in promoting RCI (Chapter 6). The first theme relates to the overriding role of the RCI subregional programs and the Pacific Community in fostering and enabling systematic, close, and sustained cooperation and RCI leadership among countries. The second, third, and fourth broadly reflect the prevailing three main strategic directions that guide RCI operations of countries and MDBs in Asia and the Pacific. The fifth is on how MDBs can innovate and strengthen their RCI assistance to individual countries and country groupings.

The collective approach through all the chapters shows (i) how the Asia and Pacific region's RCI experience and associated assistance of MDBs have helped respond to the emergency phase of the COVID-19 pandemic and beyond; (ii) what and how RCI contributes to the region's transition to recovery; (iii) emerging perspectives on how future country-led RCI, assisted by MDBs, should prioritize and deal with (a) the recovery in relation to connectivity; (b) trade, investment, and migration; and (c) regional public goods; and (iv) how countries and MDBs are evolving their participation in and support for RCI. A summary of each theme chapter is presented below.

Regional cooperation against the pandemic. The Asia Pacific Vaccine Access Facility (APVAX) helps distribute, prepare, and administer vaccines in the Philippines (photo by Eric Sales/ADB).

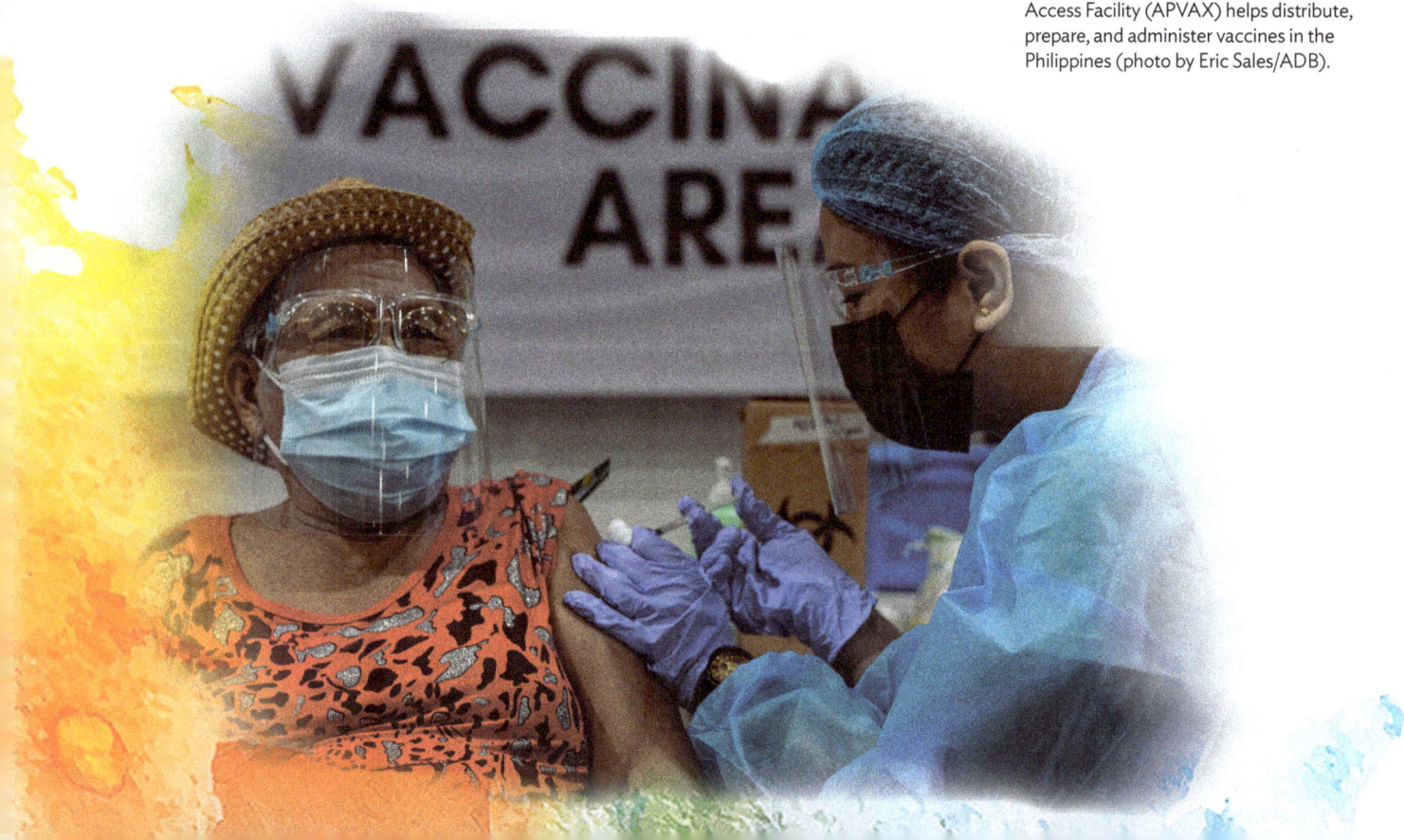

Innovation and Strengthening of Collective Action (Chapter 2)

Some pre-pandemic RCI trends and features underlay the widespread and rapid cross-border transmission of COVID-19, and some provided a ready foundation for responding to the pandemic through intercountry actions. At the outbreak of the pandemic, the Asia and Pacific region was (and still is) home to some of the world's largest cross-border flows, including people. However, regional or even subregional health systems were incomplete and had gaps in their approaches and capabilities, and cross-border sharing of health-related information was limited. Yet, the region had a good track record of effective intercountry cooperation—mainly on a subregional but also inter-subregional basis—combating outbreaks of other communicable and infectious diseases such as severe acute respiratory syndrome (SARS), avian influenza, HIV/AIDS, and tuberculosis. In the process, several MDBs provided a range of valuable technical, advisory, and financial support.

Tackling the emergency. A diverse set of regional cooperation initiatives and the directly associated MDB support reflect country-led commitment to and efforts to achieve wider-scale responses. The initiatives include interdisciplinary and multisector approaches to (i) *regional public health* (maintenance of essential health services and systems; surveillance infection prevention and control; and regional coordination, planning, and monitoring); and (ii) *trade, investment, and mobility* (keeping borders open for the flow of essential goods, supporting wider trade facilitation, sustaining inclusive economic activity in the tradable sector, and coordinating macroeconomic management and fiscal stability). MDBs provided advice and technical and financial assistance to supplement resources and strengthen capabilities of countries, and trade finance for the private sector, particularly small and medium-sized enterprises.

Easing the transition. Country-led joint initiatives and associated MDB assistance supported the "mutually beneficial transition" from emergency to recovery, following two paths. The first is activities of subregional RCI platforms to improve supply chains, build resilience to future crises, and prepare for the safe movement of people. MDBs (i) helped introduce new digital technologies and harmonize procedures and practices to support trade expansion; (ii) assisted multisector interventions to strengthen regional public health; (iii) increased South–South learning and technology sharing; and (iv) contributed to making tourism safer, more inclusive, and greener. Countries and MDBs began to strategize, identifying and introducing elements of "building back better." They considered the pre-pandemic vulnerabilities that had accumulated in the course of development over the years as well as new trends and opportunities—such as digitalization—arising as a result of new behaviors by businesses, people, and government during the emergency phase.

Vaccines—crucial to transition. The second path of "mutually beneficial transition" is vaccine distribution. While vaccination programs are almost exclusively implemented nationally, wider access to vaccines by all countries and greater national coverage of vaccination confer a regional benefit by enabling safer cross-border mobility of people. The ASEAN Comprehensive Recovery Framework, for example, supports vaccine rollout across the 10 ASEAN members. MDBs, too, have been advocating for fair access to and distribution of vaccines across Asia and the Pacific and, in some cases, have supported "pooled procurement" of vaccines on behalf of smaller economies.

Post–COVID-19 recovery. A comprehensive set of RCI initiatives are being implemented through the three subregional RCI programs and the Pacific Community. The initiatives are strategic, (i) taking medium- to longer-term knowledge-based perspectives; (ii) innovating intercountry coordination mechanisms (e.g., a new subregional development partners forum); (iii) deepening but also innovating RCI in traditional areas (e.g., *integrated* energy markets, *green* transport connectivity); (iv) widening RCI into new sector and thematic domains (e.g., economic migration, regional food safety networks, regional operating standards for specific sectors); and (v) mainstreaming new digital technologies to expand and diversify cross-borders flows (e.g., digital trade). Across all these initiatives, MDBs use not only conventional but also innovative approaches to deliver programs and projects (e.g., knowledge products on *inter-subregional* RCI).

Importance of a strategic and multisector approach. At the heart of the GMS approach is a balanced grouping of different sectors (e.g., health, environment, infrastructure, agriculture) working in tandem on complementary activities, and under an overarching framework that links the GMS's COVID-19 response and recovery plan with the GMS's long-term strategic framework 2022–2030. The response and recovery plan includes a list of priority projects under a regional investment framework to support its implementation. The projects present opportunities for development partners, including MDBs, to execute their regional operational programming in direct support of the GMS's subregional agreements to deal with COVID-19.

Lessons identified. COVID-19 has tested the strength of the Asia and Pacific region's RCI and associated MDB support to respond collectively to a far-reaching crisis. Overall, the outcomes have been meaningful and beneficial. The ongoing experience has brought to light the continuing imperative for countries and MDBs, individually and collectively, to broaden, strengthen, and deepen innovation in their approaches to comprehensive regional public health. They must achieve post–COVID-19 recovery that overcomes the preexisting vulnerabilities that put so many in the region at risk of incurring economic and social loss when the pandemic struck.

Quality Regional Connectivity (Chapter 3)

High-quality connectivity is central to "building back better" post–COVID-19 recovery. Notwithstanding that trade has rebounded from initial shocks, the pandemic has exposed the fragilities of global value chains and points to several structural challenges that need to be confronted. Connectivity supports strong regional and global trade, integrates national and cross-border infrastructure, expands the use of digital technologies as a leading driver of trade competitiveness, is more resilient in the face of stress, and enables global trade to achieve net zero transition (a balance between emissions and emission reductions). A basic premise is that the availability of high-quality connectivity infrastructure—not the relative cost of labor—will become a leading factor in how much and where future foreign direct investment is attracted across Asia and the Pacific.

Trade and connectivity resilience. Logistics innovated the use of cargo capacity and generally proved resilient, although some global and regional supply chain bottlenecks remain. Policy makers designated logistics as an essential service, exempting it from some cross-border restrictions, and stepped up interagency coordination or simplified customs processes, particularly for essential and emergency goods. By the end of 2020, global and Asian trade volume had exceeded pre-pandemic levels.

Quality infrastructure for trade and supply chains. Robust statistical analyses substantiate the interdependence of quality infrastructure and global value chains (GVCs). Quality infrastructure—national infrastructure and cross-border connectivity—enables and incentivizes GVC participation, and expanded or deepened investment in GVCs, in turn, strengthens the productivity and economic viability of investment in quality infrastructure. The reciprocal relationship becomes more positive as the quality of infrastructure increases. However, statistical analyses demonstrate that the importance or strength of the relationship may vary across different types of infrastructure, and by industry and product complexity, depending on how a measurable reduction in the quality of a type of infrastructure operates or impacts specific elements of GVC performance. An issue of much importance—and at times debated within countries and MDBs and other development finance partners—is the link between external and internal connectivity infrastructure. Results from geographic information system (GIS) analyses clearly show that substantive interdependencies are possible across various infrastructure components of a multimodal transport system that extends long distances inland from a major border trade crossing. This is increasingly true in the case of information and communication technology (ICT) infrastructure that supports digital trade in data, information, and services. From an RCI perspective, connectivity infrastructure is not confined to infrastructure in the limited area where merchandise trade flows cross a physical border. A wider geographic perspective allows policy makers to leverage investment in quality infrastructure connectivity in post–COVID-19 recovery to generate wider economic benefits across a country and mitigate national income inequality.

Rising importance and challenges of information and communication technology. ICT is a leading component of quality infrastructure for the Asia and Pacific region from positive and less positive perspectives. Positive because ICT is becoming ubiquitous, with the potential to dramatically increase the productivity of physical connectivity and logistics systems and reduce costs of trade, reduce coordination costs, diversify cross-border flows, and enable firms of almost any size to participate in regional and global trade. ICT and quality infrastructure are synonymous. Yet, a less positive feature of the rise of ICT in quality infrastructure is the large and pervasive digital divide in many parts of the region. The COVID-19 pandemic has made clear that many people and small firms find it difficult to leverage digital technology to overcome economic hardships caused by lockdowns and social distancing, and to access basic goods and services. ICT has the potential to adversely impact economic opportunities of people with less formal education and few digital skills. When planning post–COVID-19 recovery, policy makers must devote their concerted attention to preparing people to participate in an ICT-centered regional economy with quality infrastructure.

Trade policy. The outlook is both positive and less so for opportunities to build quality infrastructure in the Asia. The Regional Comprehensive Economic Partnership (RCEP) offers substantial prospects to reduce barriers to merchandise trade and create larger markets in which regional and global value chains can specialize, while offering greater economies of scale for investment in quality infrastructure. Yet, the quantity and quality of connectivity infrastructure differ greatly among RCEP members, and much digital infrastructure has limited cross-border interoperability. Policy makers planning for a robust post–COVID-19 recovery will need to try harder to promote investment in quality infrastructure, allow ICT to operate efficiently across borders, and put in place parallel agreements on trade in services not covered under RCEP. The major RCI subregional programs can continue to support subregional and inter-subregional investment and policy reform in specific connectivity infrastructure sectors where they traditionally operate. Physical infrastructure connectivity, augmented by trade and suitable policies, remain the best way forward to strengthen supply chains.

Infrastructure and net zero transition. The Asia and Pacific region needs quality infrastructure investment that helps significantly reduce greenhouse gas emissions from trade. The region must explore and consider adopting technological innovations such as carbon capture and storage. Long-distance transport of commodities exported from and imported into the region have a high carbon footprint, and even many of the region's higher-value traded manufactured goods embed significant carbon emissions because of less energy-efficient production. If carbon pricing is introduced in the region or if non-regional importers of Asia's exports introduce a carbon levy of sorts, that could raise the costs of trade for Asian manufacturers. Asia's policy makers need to encourage Asian businesses and industry in the tradable sector to invest in greener infrastructure and logistics through such approaches as achieving greater energy efficiency, using greener fuels and power sources, and relocating energy-intensive manufacturing closer to clean energy sources. And governments need to expand their support for greater cross-border trade in renewable energy, which is a nascent subsector and regional market.

Investment in quality infrastructure can contribute to a greener, resilient, and more inclusive system of trade for the future, which can continue to underpin global prosperity and offer development pathways for developing economies, including those across Asia and the Pacific. Green and connected infrastructure, together with ICT, will become the new basis of economic competitiveness to attract and anchor GVC activities.

Inclusive Trade, Investment, and Migration (Chapter 4)

Structural transformation and the distribution of gains from economic integration. A central tenet of "building back better" post–COVID-19 recovery is that the patterns of future economic integration generate wider distribution of economic benefits across society and reduce or at least mitigate economic inequality. Structural change induced by trade, investment, and migration means reallocation of resources and can create winners and losers. MDBs must assist policy makers in ensuring that trade, investment, and migration become more inclusive. Concerns about economic integration's felt or perceived inequality preceded the pandemic, and support for economic integration remains stronger in lower-income countries that have seen significant job creation and increased wages. Trade, foreign investments, and migration are linked to inequality.

Trade and inequality. Empirical analyses affirm that near- and long-term aggregate and mutual benefits are considerable for countries, industries, and firms that engage in open trade. Poverty reduction and reduced unemployment, however, are dependent on the nature and quality of policies and institutions. Various studies show that trade liberalization raised inequality in emerging markets and developing economies because of several factors. As trade often introduces more sophisticated technologies into the economy, better-educated workers earn more than those with less education. Trade is likely to become more technology and skill intensive, and wage differentials across firms widened as exporting firms raised wages faster than non-exporters. Reallocating workers who have lost their jobs in disrupted industries can be slow and costly, constraining workers' access to new jobs in expanding sectors and leading to long unemployment. The benefits and losses from trade are often geographically concentrated in clusters of firms, leading to greater spatial inequalities within countries.

Investment and inequality. As open trade induced the rise of regional and global value chains, it also led to extraordinary inflows of foreign direct investment (FDI), which raised the productivity of local firms and industries and increased product complexity. The presence of foreign firms can be associated with the introduction of higher workplace standards and more diverse forms of preferred worker compensation. Yet, foreign investment can also accentuate the outcomes of technological change on the distribution of income by, for example, increasing the wage gap between skilled and unskilled workers, where younger, more highly educated workers are more likely to be employed by a foreign firm under permanent contracts. In many economies, FDI in greenfield investment projects has become more technology and skill intensive and less labor-intensive, creating fewer jobs per dollar invested. Geographical inequality results as FDI in greenfield projects in specific sectors is increasingly clustered and, in the case of services, increasingly located in already higher-income cities or other urban centers.

Migration and inequality. The literature on the relationship between migration and inequality is limited and the results mixed. The relationship may well change as a source country's pool of outbound migrants becomes more diverse or inclusive in terms of education, skills, income, and gender, increasing income equality. An analysis of household survey data bears out this assumption, revealing that in countries with a short migration history, higher-income people are more likely than the poor to say they intend to migrate. In countries with longer migration experience, however, interest in migrating is more evenly distributed across the population. Another factor supporting the view that migration increases income equality is that remittances are more stable over time and across changes in a country's economic cycle than trade and FDI flows, and they can cushion the impact of economic loss from disasters triggered by natural hazards or sudden economic disruption at home. However, data confirm that the COVID-19 pandemic resulted in migrant job losses and remittances in Asia and the Pacific, albeit with notable differences across countries.

Policies to promote inclusive trade, investment, and migration. Cross-border economic integration delivers productivity growth, and gains from trade and foreign investments can be amplified by policies that foster trade and investment openness and facilitate trade. Other policies are needed, however, to ensure that growth from open trade, investment, and migration is inclusive, and that gains can be widely shared. MDBs should support and coordinate a diverse policy agenda by advising on policy and enabling exchange of experiences and know-how across countries. Policy areas include (i) strengthening of social safety nets, education, and training to ease labor mobility; (ii) public investments in infrastructure and logistics to encourage private investment in lagging regions; (iii) programs that foster linkages between foreign-sponsored production facilities and local suppliers; and (iv) strong alignment of trade and foreign investment with the country's skill base.

Regional Approaches to Support Air Pollution Management in South Asia (Chapter 5)

A World Bank study shows how important it is to have deep understanding and appreciation of complex, technical, and economic dimensions of a major development issue in regional public goods (air pollution) to identify cross-border solutions and instigate collective action. Successful national actions are complementary and even a precursor to viable intercountry actions. The research's new findings allow air quality policy makers to better evaluate the environmental effectiveness of policy measures and the conditions in which cross-jurisdictional cooperation is appropriate.

Regional challenge to provide clean air. South Asia faces a continuing threat to public health from ambient (outdoor) air pollution, which causes about 17% of all deaths in South Asia. Close to 95% of South Asians live where ambient fine particulate matter ($PM_{2.5}$) concentrations exceed the World Health Organization (WHO) Air Quality Guideline. Of the top 20 cities in the world with the poorest air quality in 2016, 17 were in South Asia. The associated annual cost of health damages in South Asian countries is about 1.5%–10.6% of gross domestic product (GDP) equivalent.

Air quality management in South Asia. South Asian countries have strengthened their air quality management (AQM) programs, but more work is required. Recent years have seen various policy responses to deal with air pollution, including the draft Bangladesh Clean Air Act, the National Electrical Vehicles Policy in Pakistan, and India's National Clean Air Programme. They will allow economies to grow without a corresponding increase in air pollution. However, beyond the decoupling efforts, further measures will be required to reduce particulate pollution to a level that will achieve WHO's first interim target for $PM_{2.5}$ emissions.

Regional "airshed" approach. Highly diverse sources and locations of air pollution underline the complexity of air pollution in South Asia. Air pollution management has largely centered on cities, considering fixed or mobile sources within a given spatial area or administrative boundary such as a city or municipal region. However, from a technical and policy perspective, the concept of "airsheds" is more useful to better understand the sources and impacts of air pollution and to design meaningful responses rather than limit them within administrative boundaries. The airshed as a planning and management tool is similar to the watershed for water resources, although air pollution is more demanding to sample from different "nonpoint" sources. Regional cooperation, therefore, is even more important because the effects of air pollution frequently cross borders.

Given the multisector nature of air pollution sources in South Asia, effective AQM must also focus on other sources, such as household energy uses and small industries. Four alternative AQM options could improve air quality and bring population exposure closer to international air quality standards. Differing in quantity and regional distribution of exposure improvements and in cost-effectiveness, the four options or scenarios are (i) "ad hoc selection of measures," which assesses upscaling of measures being taken in parts of South Asia to the whole Asia and Pacific region; (ii) "maximum technically feasible emission reduction," which explores the range of air quality improvements that could be achieved in 2030 by fully implementing all currently available technical emission controls; (iii) a more targeted approach, using which AQM could focus on pollution hot spots in South Asia and bring mean population exposure to $PM_{2.5}$ in each region in compliance with WHO interim target 1; and (iv) cost-effective cuts of harmful population exposure to $PM_{2.5}$ through a common but differentiated approach coordinated across South Asia.

A regionally coordinated solution—the most cost-effective. *The most cost-effective air quality improvements emerge from a common but differentiated move to the WHO interim targets coordinated across South Asia.* If each region cut exposure below the next lower interim target, mean exposure in South Asia would decline by 40% below 2018 levels, at about $5.7 billion per year, i.e., 0.11% of GDP, 45% lower than those of the "ad hoc selection of measures" strategy. The study concludes that cost-effective AQM requires airshed-wide intercountry coordination through cross-jurisdictional mechanisms. Cost-effectiveness can be balanced across regions in a way that maximizes cost savings and shared benefits from airshed-wide coordination.

Multilateral Development Banks as Key Partners Promoting Regional Cooperation and Integration (Chapter 6)

Cooperation as a major determinant of development resilience. Two closely related premises are that *cooperation is a major determinant of economic resilience, and, when it comes to the COVID-19 pandemic and its associated economic crisis, the global consequences of the crisis require interregional cooperation.* MDBs are not only independent development finance institutions with some unique characteristics but also a system of multilateral partners whose common purpose of helping countries (including many common member states) end the pandemic and recover brings them into close and complementary alignment on operational approaches and methods. Given their multilateral character, MDBs are in a preferred position among development finance agencies to foster multistakeholder (government, private sector, civil society) cooperation that can resolve the complexity of cross-border challenges.

Multilateral development bank mandates, roles, strategies, and instruments to support regional cooperation and integration. The five MDBs are similar but also distinct, particularly the Islamic Development Bank (IsDB), with its unique membership structure—only from the Global South—which adds a strong element of solidarity to the bank's support for intercountry cooperation. IsDB's RCI strategy mandates *that the organization itself be "a primary connecting platform"* for its member countries, regional cooperation organizations, and communities to cooperate with each other. MDBs use a wide array of investment, policy, and knowledge-based instruments to support RCI in their member countries. IsDB demonstrates how an MDB consisting of several distinct entities (in relation to sovereign investment, nonsovereign investment, trade finance, insurance and export credit, training and capacity building, knowledge sharing) executes various RCI-type programs to achieve a highly complementary approach to RCI in an individual member country or subregion. For example, IsDB has pioneered the highly innovative reverse linkages mechanism, which operates between subregions and within them for peer-to-peer cooperation to design innovative sector and thematic solutions and build capacity to make them sustainable.

Broadening participation in multilateral development banks' regional cooperation and integration operations. Notwithstanding the RCI successes achieved by MDBs drawing on their diverse operational approaches and capabilities, civil society, private businesses of all sizes, academia and other centers of excellence, new and more sector and subsector regional cooperation entities, and subnational sovereign actors must participate more in RCI. MDBs should make greater efforts to expedite wider participation from below in their existing RCI operations to help innovate new models, open new channels to resolve cross-border issues (e.g., vaccine delivery), and mobilize new resources for RCI. Doing so is essential if RCI is to contribute to inclusive post–COVID-19 recovery and to overcome preexisting inequalities, especially those aggravated by the pandemic.

Management of COVID-19. The chapter discusses the scope, types, and significance of COVID-19 response interventions undertaken by MDBs and how (albeit, after some initial coordination challenges) countries and MDBs collaborated to ensure essential cross-border flows and to deliver vital social protection, including to those in the tradable sector. The programs have benefited households, health workers, and small and medium-sized enterprises, among other disadvantaged or vulnerable groups.

Digitalization and innovative financing imperatives. The Asia and Pacific region must bridge the digital divide and mainstream digitalization of connectivity, logistics, and trade facilitation systems into the cross-border financial system. Assistance is imperative to enable a smooth and inclusive transition for the workforce segment adversely impacted by the resulting economic structural transformation.

Islamic finance. Islamic finance plays a significant and beneficial role in development finance. It combines philanthropy, profit and loss sharing, and revenue-generating financing that can be used to expand access to financial services and promote socially responsible investment. Cooperation between MDBs and between MDBs and regional cooperation organizations could help Islamic finance grow and lead to international agreements on regulatory and operational standards for it. Countries and regions could then access a larger pool of financing to build COVID-19 recovery and help mitigate conventional financial risks that can lead to wider financial shocks.

The five theme chapters together provide readers with (i) substantial empirical evidence on how countries and MDBs responded with RCI activities, making use of Asia and the Pacific's established subregional RCI platforms; (ii) a rich set of RCI-related research findings and their implications for design and prioritization of and investment in large RCI projects, as well as a range of policy reforms; (iii) a window to the complexity of creating a critical regional and global public good that must consider national and cross-border features and challenges; and (iv) lessons that could increase the efficacy of MDBs' support for RCI in Asia and the Pacific and even elsewhere.

Readers, be they established RCI practitioners or new to RCI, are strongly encouraged to consider how the findings may be used to advance their own important RCI work or evolving interest in greater regional cooperation, to end the COVID-19 emergency and support strong recovery for all countries and people of Asia and the Pacific.

References

Asia Regional Integration Center. Chiang Mai Initiative [Multilateralisation].

Asian Development Bank (ADB). 2018. Estimating the Impact of Regional Integration on Economic Growth and Poverty Reduction. *Asian Economic Integration Report 2018*. Manila. pp. 12–4.

———. 2020. An Updated Assessment of the Economic Impact of COVID-19. *ADB Briefs*. 133.

ADB, United Nations Development Programme, and United Nations Economic and Social Commission for Asia and the Pacific. 2021. *Responding to the COVID-19 Pandemic: Leaving No Country Behind*. Bangkok.

2 Innovating and Strengthening Cross-Border Collective Action

Working together in a crisis can mean working differently. Countries and multilateral development banks quickly reprioritized and reprogrammed their country and cross-border development plans and programs and reallocated resources accordingly.

Highlights

Paramount role of country leadership and experience. Country leadership, experience, commitment, and sustained cooperation are key to enabling Asia and the Pacific to tackle a global and regional crisis and achieve mutually beneficial development outcomes. To deal with the coronavirus disease (COVID-19) emergency, countries acted collectively, drawing upon their experience and lessons learned from earlier regional public health crises.

Regional and subregional cooperation platforms were critical in galvanizing collective action. Whether focused on policy coordination (e.g., Association of Southeast Asian Nations, South Asian Association for Regional Cooperation Program) or on operations (e.g., Greater Mekong Subregion Program, South Asia Subregional Economic Cooperation Program, Central Asia Regional Economic Cooperation Program), the platforms enabled countries to quickly rally members to respond to the COVID-19 crisis and to link national, regional, and global coordination and actions. Regional coordination and cooperation across subregional platforms develop the complementarity needed to underpin a strategy of timely, coordinated, and cohesive responses to a regional health crisis and to create and apply innovations widely and quickly.

Multilateral development banks (MDBs) supported countries' efforts in unique and effective ways. MDBs, as key development partners, brought a unique blend of country-specific and cross-border experience, knowledge and capabilities, and resources, which have been deployed to support countries' own and collective efforts.

Countries and MDBs innovated, adapted, and took national and joint action quickly to face the emergency. Working together in a crisis can mean working differently. Countries and MDBs quickly reprioritized and reprogrammed their country and cross-border development plans and programs and reallocated resources accordingly. MDBs applied existing business processes in innovative ways and introduced new ones.

Equitable national vaccination is a regional public good and enables region-wide recovery. MDBs have assisted countries with equitable procurement and regional access to vaccines and eased trade to expedite timely, cost-effective vaccine delivery. Every vaccinee reduces the health risks for everyone else and lowers the risks that accompany cross-border movement of people.

Regional cooperation should be sustained through transition and recovery. Building on their successes and accomplishments in 2020 and 2021, countries should continue acting collectively to get through the emergency and achieve full post–COVID-19 recovery. Reaching the 2030 Sustainable Development Goals requires regional cooperation and integration to generate mutually beneficial inclusive and sustainable growth, maintain national and cross-border security, and develop regional perspectives to amplify the Asian voice in the global community.

Introduction

Sudden and significant economic and social impacts from the onset of the COVID-19 pandemic signaled the need for countries across the Asia and Pacific region to coordinate and cooperate closely with each other. Looking to their successful regional initiatives to beat back avian influenza, HIV/AIDS, severe acute respiratory syndrome (SARS), and tuberculosis, countries embarked on another collective and cooperative path to defend themselves against COVID-19 in early 2020.

MDBs are well-placed to help countries achieve health security as a regional public good. MDBs can support knowledge work and knowledge sharing, leading to improved and closely aligned health policy and regulatory frameworks among countries. Developing common health protocols and information-sharing platforms to identify, surveil, diagnose, and treat disease and to mobilize financial resources are the hallmarks of collaboration.

This chapter explains the crucial role of country-led regional cooperation and integration (RCI) and attendant collective action in dealing with the COVID-19 pandemic and of the associated functions and support of MDBs.[4] The chapter focuses on cross-border initiatives and activities undertaken through four subregional economic cooperation platforms.[5]

---

[4] In this chapter, the Asian Development Bank (ADB) is the primary reference source for MDBs. Unless specified, the chapter uses a generic description of actual and potential MDB support for RCI and collective action, given MDBs' shared commitment to RCI.

[5] The Central Asia Regional Economic Cooperation (CAREC) (Afghanistan, Azerbaijan, the People's Republic of China [PRC], Georgia, Kazakhstan, the Kyrgyz Republic, Mongolia, Pakistan, Tajikistan, Turkmenistan, and Uzbekistan); the Greater Mekong Subregion (GMS) (Cambodia, the PRC [Yunnan Province and Guangxi Zhuang Autonomous Region], the Lao People's Democratic Republic, Myanmar, Thailand, and Viet Nam); the South Asia Subregional Economic Cooperation (SASEC) (Bangladesh, Bhutan, India, Maldives, Myanmar, Nepal, and Sri Lanka); and the Pacific Islands Forum (PIF) (Australia, Cook Islands, the Federated States of Micronesia, Fiji, French Polynesia, Kiribati, Nauru, New Caledonia, New Zealand, Niue, Palau, Papua New Guinea, the Republic of Marshall Islands, Samoa, Solomon Islands, Tonga, Tuvalu, and Vanuatu). PIF leaders have established the Council of Regional Organisations of the Pacific (CROP) to improve cooperation, coordination, and collaboration among intergovernmental regional organizations to achieve sustainable development. ADB placed on hold its assistance in Afghanistan effective 15 August 2021. https://www.adb.org/news/adb-statement-afghanistan.

Foundations for Action: Pre–COVID-19 Cooperation in Combating Pandemics and Securing Regional Health

The Asia and Pacific region is home to some of the world's largest intra- and interregional movement of goods, services, business travelers, and labor across many borders (Figure 2), making regional health security a paramount regional public good. National and regional cooperation and collective action on health are essential. Achieving health security as a regional public good depends on sustained cross-border cooperation on government-led decisions and activities, supported by countries' public and private resources and complementary support from development partners, including MDBs.

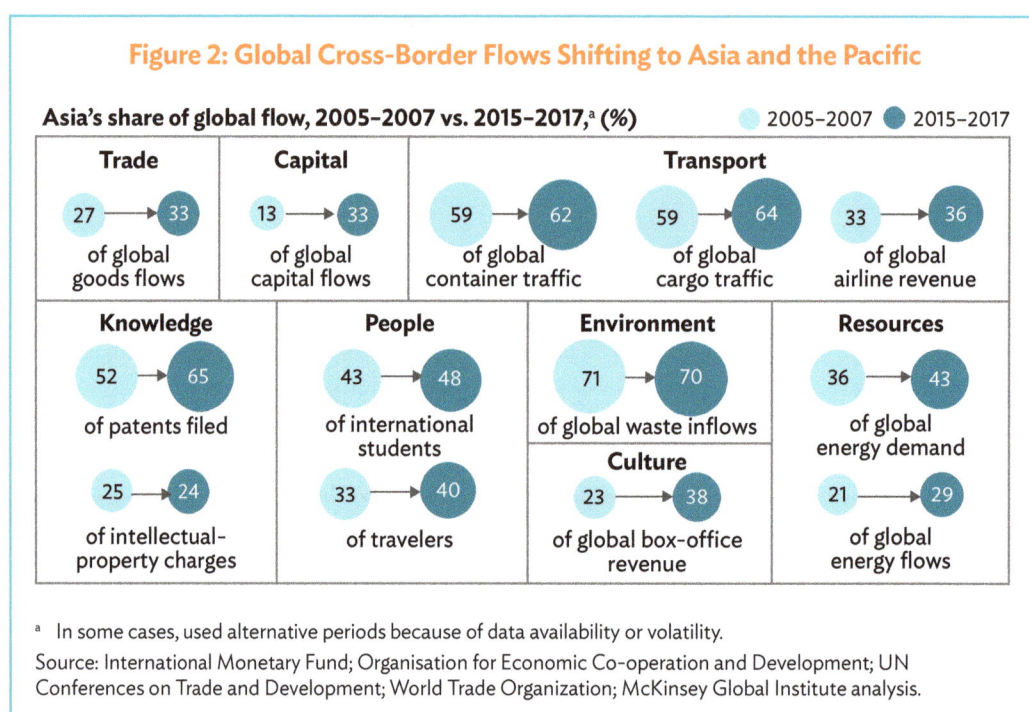

Figure 2: Global Cross-Border Flows Shifting to Asia and the Pacific

Asia's share of global flow, 2005–2007 vs. 2015–2017,[a] (%)   ● 2005–2007 ● 2015–2017

Trade	Capital	Transport		
27 → 33	13 → 33	59 → 62	59 → 64	33 → 36
of global goods flows	of global capital flows	of global container traffic	of global cargo traffic	of global airline revenue

Knowledge	People	Environment	Resources
52 → 65	43 → 48	71 → 70	36 → 43
of patents filed	of international students	of global waste inflows	of global energy demand
25 → 24	33 → 40	**Culture** 23 → 38	21 → 29
of intellectual-property charges	of travelers	of global box-office revenue	of global energy flows

[a] In some cases, used alternative periods because of data availability or volatility.

Source: International Monetary Fund; Organisation for Economic Co-operation and Development; UN Conferences on Trade and Development; World Trade Organization; McKinsey Global Institute analysis.

Since the early 2000s, countries in the Asia and Pacific region have successfully implemented projects combating national and cross-border spread of communicable and infectious diseases (e.g., SARS, avian flu, HIV/AIDS, tuberculosis), achieving positive results in regional health security (ADB 2018). The interventions provided countries and MDBs with valuable knowledge and experience to draw upon to respond quickly and effectively to the COVID-19 pandemic. They recognized, for example, the need for flexible program and project implementation arrangements; a focus on immediate and near-term needs of developing member countries (DMCs) (hospital equipment, training, and communication programs) to enable early and effective communicable disease control; multisector collaboration across organizations; and effective regional vaccine delivery (Box 1). The interventions linked national and intercountry strategies, used innovations, shared knowledge, gave countries access to higher technologies, and developed capacity (Figure 3).

Box 1: Strengthening Systems for Effective Coverage of New Vaccines in the Pacific

In 2018, an Asian Development Bank (ADB)–assisted project supported joint procurement of vaccines and their delivery to targeted groups in the Pacific. Systems Strengthening for Effective Coverage of New Vaccines in the Pacific employs a regional approach to bolstering critical components of health systems for improved immunization outcomes by introducing three vaccines in four Pacific island countries: Samoa, Tonga, Tuvalu, and Vanuatu. Pooled—that is, regional—procurement through the United Nations Children's Fund (UNICEF) allows countries to benefit from lower prices, quality products, and technical expertise in vaccines and cold chain management and in management of emergency stockpiles.

Source: ADB. 2018. *Proposed Loan and Grants. Independent State of Samoa, Kingdom of Tonga, Tuvalu, and Republic of Vanuatu: Systems Strengthening for Effective Coverage of New Vaccines in the Pacific Project*. Manila.

Figure 3: Greater Mekong Subregion Health Security Project, 2017–2022

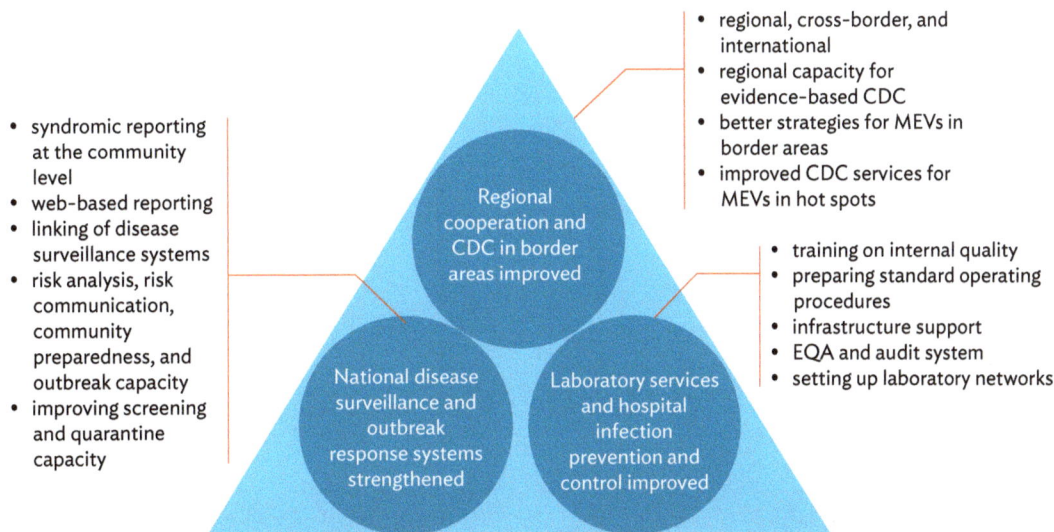

- syndromic reporting at the community level
- web-based reporting
- linking of disease surveillance systems
- risk analysis, risk communication, community preparedness, and outbreak capacity
- improving screening and quarantine capacity

Regional cooperation and CDC in border areas improved

National disease surveillance and outbreak response systems strengthened

Laboratory services and hospital infection prevention and control improved

- regional, cross-border, and international
- regional capacity for evidence-based CDC
- better strategies for MEVs in border areas
- improved CDC services for MEVs in hot spots

- training on internal quality
- preparing standard operating procedures
- infrastructure support
- EQA and audit system
- setting up laboratory networks

CDC = communicable disease control; EQA = external quality assessment; MEVs = migrant and mobile people, ethnic minorities, and other vulnerable groups.
Source: Asian Development Bank.

Immediate Response to the COVID-19 Emergency: Benefits of Cross-Border Collective Action

Notwithstanding earlier accomplishments, the rapid spread of the COVID-19 pandemic highlighted that national health systems, regional coordination, and global arrangements remained incomplete. While countries in Asia acted quickly to respond to the emergency, gaps clearly existed, such as inadequate resources to strengthen outbreak response, lack of up-to-date scientific and economic data, and little medical research to support decision-making. Responses need to go beyond health to include complementary contributions from other sectors, reflecting the links between human, animal, and environmental health.

Against this background, the region's management of the pandemic required commitment and action to widely coordinate national responses and develop and implement activities reflecting interdisciplinary and multisector approaches. The Central Asia Regional Economic Cooperation (CAREC), the Greater Mekong Subregion (GMS), the South Asia Subregional Economic Cooperation (SASEC), and the Pacific Islands Forum (PIF) and Council of Regional Organisations of the Pacific (CROP), with assistance from MDBs and other development partners, responded to the emergency with vital and innovative initiatives.

Regional public health. Countries and MDBs agreed that acting jointly was paramount to combat the spread of the virus (nationally and across borders) and to detect and treat the infected. Subregional RCI platforms such as GMS, CAREC, and PIF have actively assisted the smooth flow of essential goods and services; infection surveillance, prevention, and control; and/or regional coordination, planning, and monitoring. MDBs provided advice and technical and financial assistance to strengthen countries' capabilities (Table 2).

A clinic in Mongolia. The Protecting Health Status of Poor during Financial Crisis Project provides the poor free access to essential health services necessary to mitigate the impact of the financial crisis (photo by Eric Sales/ADB).

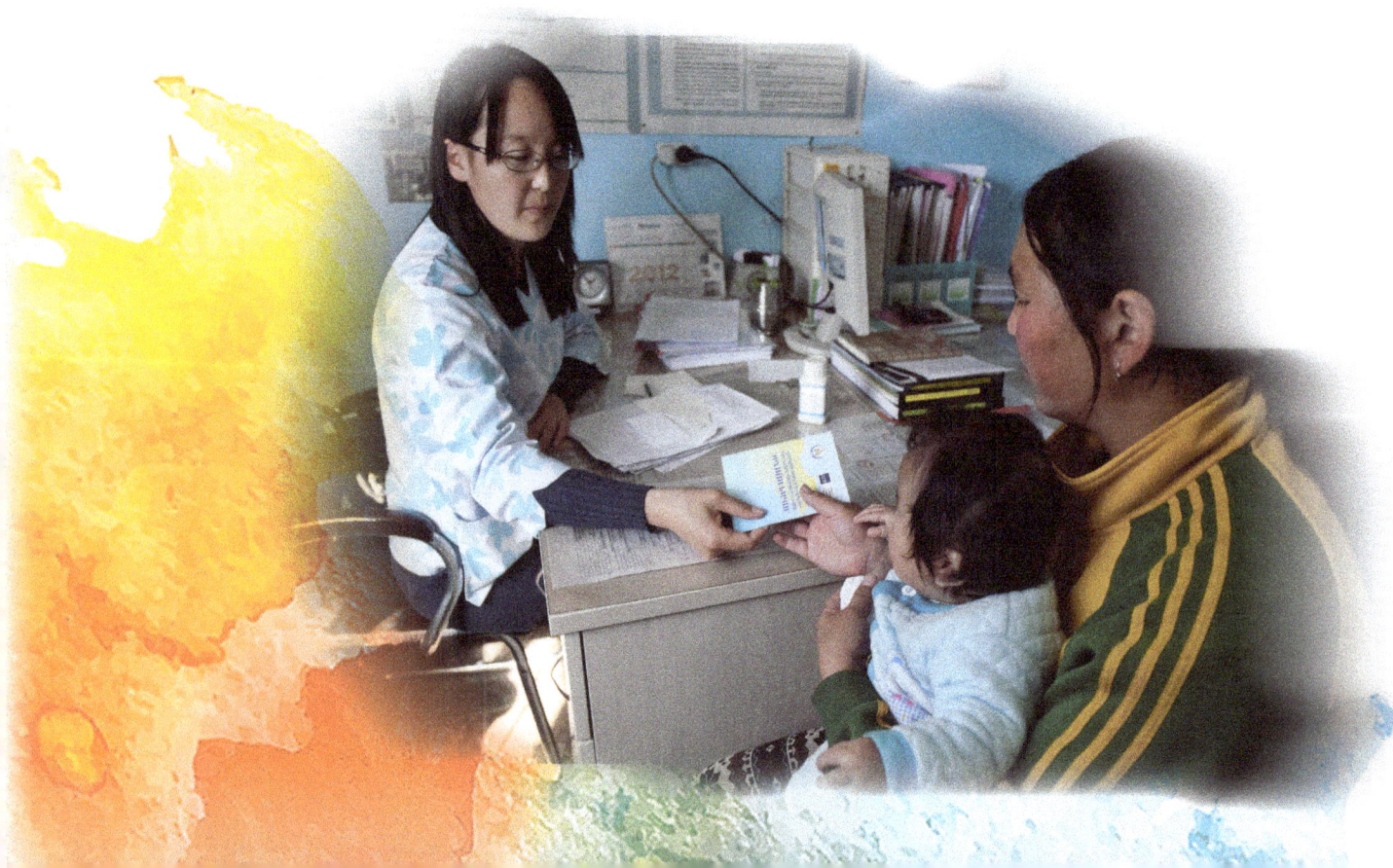

Table 2: Regional Public Health

Areas of Collective Action	Subregional/Country-Led Initiatives	Multilateral Development Bank Support
• Maintaining essential health services and systems • Surveillance, infection prevention and control • Regional coordination, planning, and monitoring	The Pacific Islands Forum established the Pacific Humanitarian Pathway on COVID-19 (PHP-C), which coordinates the intercountry movement of medical supplies, technical experts, supported regional task force. GMS Working Group on Health Cooperation "extraordinary meeting (Feb 2020) for planning effective responses to COVID-19 both at the regional and country levels, and coordination with the ASEAN Secretariat. The working group mobilized networks from ongoing (MDB-assisted) GMS health security projects for a rapid response to the pandemic. CAREC-wide daily reporting of new cases, sharing information on COVID-19 practice, and intercountry provision of medical teams and relief equipment. CAREC health working group to support health cooperation.	Grant financing for COVID-19 testing kits. Emergency response loans for the health service sectors. Contribution to COVAX (e.g., APVAX) Emergency response loans to raise capacity of health systems to WHO standards, regional information sharing and surveillance on health. TA for the health systems' resilience and capacity for epidemic response and procurement of diagnostic and laboratory equipment. MDB-initiated CAREC health scoping study identifying key areas for regional cooperation. Regional TA to address regional health threats, including formulating a CAREC health strategy for improving health systems and health security capacities.

APVAX = Asia Pacific Vaccine Access Facility, ASEAN = Association of Southeast Asian Nations, CAREC = Central Asia Regional Economic Cooperation, COVAX = COVID-19 Vaccine Global Access, COVID-19 = coronavirus disease, GMS = Greater Mekong Subregion, MDB = multilateral development bank, TA = technical assistance.

Source: Asian Development Bank.

Trade, investment, and mobility. The COVID-19 outbreak required countries and regions to minimize disruptions to trade, investment, and mobility of people. Countries have acted together to ensure access to essential medical goods and services and basic food supplies. Subregional platforms such as CAREC, PIF, and SASEC were indispensable in keeping borders open, sustaining inclusive economic activities, and bolstering fiscal and macroeconomic management. MDBs provided knowledge, technical services, and financing for crisis responses and trade facilitation, mainly to support the continued participation of small and medium-sized enterprises (SMEs) in regional and global supply chains, maintain macroeconomic and financial sector stability, and promote economic recovery (Table 3). MDB-supported trade finance for the private sector helped ensure seamless, affordable transactions for firms, including SMEs. For example, from 1 April 2020 to 30 April 2021, ADB's Trade Finance Program supported more than 7,700 transactions valued at $6.9 billion.

Planning for Mutually Beneficial Transition

Transitioning from emergency to recovery. While combating the COVID-19 emergency was critical, it was vital that MDBs help countries plan and implement actions to revive the economy (Box 2). Subregional RCI platforms such as SASEC and GMS were essential to improve supply chains, build resilience to future crises, and prepare for the safe movement of people. MDBs helped introduce new digital technologies and harmonize procedures and practices during the emergency to expand trade. MDBs supported multisector interventions to encourage collaboration on regional public health. MDBs have helped reinvent regional tourism to make it safer, more inclusive, and greener. Tourism offers excellent potential for growth and its recovery is a priority in the Pacific (Table 3).

Table 3: Transitioning from Emergency to Recovery

Areas of Collective Action	Subregional and Country-Led Initiatives	Multilateral Development Bank Support
Improving supply chain and/or trade facilitation resilience	Virtual meeting of the SASEC Customs Subgroup on 30 September 2020. Agreed to develop an action plan for resiliency and preparedness of customs authorities to cope with emergencies.	Knowledge and technical support for reduction of cost of international trade of essential goods; simplified procedures and documents; digitalization of trade facilitation processes; worker safety protocols, and business continuity.
Building resilience to future crisis	GMS working groups on agriculture and environment planning for COVID-19–responsive green agribusiness supply chains, and livestock health and safety measures; integrating climate and disaster resilience into COVID-19 recovery efforts.	Technical assistance for the GMS Sustainable Agriculture and Food Security Program and the GMS Climate Change and Environmental Sustainability Program.
Enabling and preparing for safe movement of people	GMS Tourism Working Group. CAREC Tourism Strategy 2030, to facilitate safe and resilient tourism development.	Assistance on the tourism sector strategy through regional tourism standards, new safety and hygiene standards, training for tourism SMEs, preparing tourism recovery policy briefs and communications plans.

CAREC = Central Asia Regional Economic Cooperation, COVID-19 = coronavirus disease, GMS = Greater Mekong Subregion, SASEC = South Asia Subregional Economic Cooperation, SMEs = small and medium-sized enterprises.
Source: Asian Development Bank.

Box 2: The Association of Southeast Asian Nations Comprehensive Recovery Framework

The Association of Southeast Asian Nations (ASEAN) Comprehensive Recovery Framework (ACRF) was adopted at the 37th ASEAN Summit, held virtually on 12 November 2020, chaired by Viet Nam. ACRF and its implementation plan serve as a strategy and coordinating mechanism for efforts to recover from the coronavirus disease (COVID-19), enabling ASEAN to become more resilient and stronger in the aftermath of the COVID-19 crisis, considering the circumstances of the hardest-hit sectors and vulnerable groups. ACRF focuses on five expansive strategies: (i) improving the health system, (ii) strengthening human security, (iii) maximizing the potential of the intra-ASEAN market and broader economic integration, (iv) accelerating inclusive digital transformation, and (v) advancing to a more sustainable and resilient future. The summit emphasized that the success of ACRF will entail support and contributions from many stakeholders, internal and external.

Source: ASEAN. 2020. Chairman's Statement of the 37th ASEAN Summit: Cohesive and Responsive.

Sustaining a shared vision. A multisector and multicountry approach is vital to maximize the development effectiveness of any cross-border and collective anti–COVID-19 initiative. Adaptability; inclusiveness; ability to balance short-, medium-, and long-term horizons; and possession of regional leadership are essential to a subregion's future, COVID-19 notwithstanding. The Pacific Community Transition Plan 2021, for example, upholds the

Blue Pacific identity, reinforcing the promise of shared stewardship of the Pacific Ocean and reaffirming the bond of Pacific peoples with their natural resources, environment, cultures, and livelihoods (Box 3).

Box 3: The Pacific Community Transition Plan 2021: Build Resilience and Move Forward by Design, Not Disaster

Coronavirus disease (COVID-19) impacts shifted the attention and priorities of the Pacific Community, which had to quickly adapt and pivot its 10-year strategic plan to include the 12-month Transition Plan for 2021: Foundations for a Resilient Future starting in January 2021. The plan responds to recovery and "building resilience *by design*, not disaster." The plan was informed by COVID-19 assessments, national sustainable development plans, and the Pacific Community's ongoing regional commitments. It incorporates the outcomes of dialogues held with Pacific youth on their aspirations and leverages the scientific and technical expertise of staff to inform foresight activities that frame potential national and regional scenarios for the organization and its members. Guided by the Blue Pacific vision, the plan identifies four goals and six focus areas, all interconnected by sustainable systems and climate action.

Goal 1	Goal 2	Goal 3	Goal 3
Pacific people benefit from sustainable economic development	Pacific communities are empowered and resilient	Pacific people reach their potential and live long and healthy lives	One SPC delivering integrated programs through streamlined services

SPC = Pacific Community (formerly South Pacific Commission).
Source: Foundations for Change: Members Endorse SPC's 2021 Transition Plan | The Pacific Community.

Knowledge products. MDBs provided valuable knowledge products and support for knowledge services during the pandemic, such as knowledge sharing among national research and testing laboratories (Box 4); analyses of the impacts on the region's GDP, domestic demand, and employment; and setting of a forward-looking RCI agenda on economic migration and remittances (Box 5). MDBs analyzed the sources of bottlenecks in personal protective equipment, raw materials, machinery, geographic concentration of manufacturers, and export bans. MDB knowledge products have been aligned with the region's needs to monitor cross-border activities during the pandemic. For example, ADB's *Asian Economic Integration Report 2021* (ADB 2021a) examined how the pandemic impacted the region's global and regional trade and investment activities and regional and country remittances and tourism. The Asian Economic Integration Report shed light on the enormous economic potential that digitalization can unlock and policy options to bridge the digital divide across and within countries.

Box 4: The Islamic Development Bank's Reverse Linkage Interventions: Supporting Regional Coordination and Cooperation during the COVID-19 Pandemic

As part of its Strategic Preparedness and Response Program, the Islamic Development Bank (IsDB) scaled up its reverse linkage interventions to support its member countries' regional coordination efforts during the pandemic. A peer-to-peer South–South cooperation modality, the reverse linkage mechanism had been used extensively by IsDB to ease the transfer of knowledge and expertise among partnering institutions long before the pandemic. But the pandemic witnessed the wide-scale use of the modality to connect countries with each other.

Under the reverse linkage mechanism, IsDB initiated a program to build the capacities of national laboratories in its member countries whereby, for example, a network of 10 laboratories shared knowledge and best practices for surveillance and testing. Within the program's framework, the People's Republic of China is cooperating with IsDB to build the capacity of public health laboratories in eligible countries.

Another reverse linkage project was initiated between Indonesia and Singapore on artificial intelligence and advanced analytics to contain the coronavirus disease (COVID-19). The goal is to contribute to Indonesia's efforts to equip itself with robust and effective data center infrastructure to mitigate not only the COVID-19 pandemic but also possible health crises by providing comprehensive and timely data analysis. IsDB supported a reverse linkage project between Jordan and Singapore to strengthen Jordanian institutions' technical and technological capacities to produce N95 masks, not only for the COVID-19 pandemic but also for other medical purposes.

Source: IsDB.

Box 5: A Call for Bolder Regional Cooperation to Support and Protect Economic Migrants in Asia and the Pacific

Improve and strengthen the quality of health systems and associated infrastructure to ensure that mobility is pandemic-proof. The region's health systems need to better respond to health emergencies with superior medical facilities and better-skilled personnel. The pandemic has affirmed the need for higher-quality, more-reachable sanitation and water supply infrastructure.

Strengthen social protection for economic migrants. The lack of cross-border agreements may prevent migrant workers from maintaining their earned and acquired benefits. Policy options may include incorporating social security provisions into bilateral labor agreements, adopting measures to ensure equality of treatment or establishing national minimum social protections for migrant workers, and streamlining procedures and processes to make social protection portable or enable workers to access new sources of social protection.

Expand industry and profession coverage in regional agreements on mutual recognition of skills and professional qualifications. Countries are participating more in megaregional and interregional trade and investment agreements. Industries and firms will become increasingly dependent on flexible regional labor markets that allow a remarkably diverse pool of highly productive labor to cross borders in response to market demand. The preferred way to achieve the objective is through multilateral agreements on mutual recognition of skills and professional qualifications.

Protect economic migrants. They might face a wide range of firm and household employment conditions that are menacing, abusive, and even life-threatening. Policy and regulatory gaps or weak enforcement of worker protection frameworks in destination countries might push economic migrants from contracted labor arrangements into forced ones.

Strengthen the development impacts of remittances. For many countries in the region, remittances are a substantial and regular cross-border financial inflow. The functioning of financial markets can be improved to reduce fees on remittance services, especially for small transfers made by lower-income migrants. Reducing remittance costs and improving access by migrants and their families to the financial system will encourage greater use of formal channels.

Establish regional migrant information infrastructure. It can leverage new technology to efficiently share accurate, relevant, and timely migrant information; help countries apply migration best practices; and help policy makers better assess migration issues.

Source: Asian Development Bank (2021a).

Transition in Focus: Vaccine Distribution as a Regional Public Good

Vaccines provide essential regional public goods. It is in everyone's interest to be vaccinated for personal and shared benefits. The shared benefits are economic productivity and social welfare gained from reducing the risk of transmitting or contracting the disease. Every accredited vaccine allows individuals, communities, countries, and regions to avoid the worst health risks and adverse outcomes and reduce the virus's transmission. Everyone everywhere should get vaccinated as quickly as possible. The sooner that happens, the sooner the tradable sector of every economy in the region can reboot and cross-border flows of people resume. Multilateral development assistance for RCI enables the entire region to achieve mutually beneficial objectives and realize the public good (Box 6).

Box 6: Expediting Efficient Cross-Border Logistics for COVID-19 Vaccines

The Asian Development Bank (ADB) convened a webinar, Facilitating Efficient Cross-Border Logistics for COVID-19 Vaccines, on 4 February 2021 to support member countries of the South Asia Subregional Economic Cooperation (SASEC) in preparing for coronavirus disease (COVID-19) vaccine distribution and logistics. The webinar discussed issues, key actions, and next steps to expedite efficient cross-border COVID-19 vaccine logistics and presented the private sector perspective. Participants stressed the importance of sustained operational and cross-border coordination and communication, the need for uniform capacity building, and the use of regional and global resources and best practices. The event's 96 participants included senior officials from SASEC customs administrations and officials from SASEC government agencies overseeing civil aviation, foreign affairs, health, and pharmaceuticals.

Source: Asian Development Bank.

Linking national vaccination programs to regional actions creates unique health impacts. National vaccination programs against COVID-19 are a regional public good, exemplifying that national activities have critical regional and global effects. ADB's *Asian Economic Integration Report 2018: Toward Optimal Provision of Regional Public Goods in Asia and the Pacific* argues that provision of regional public goods is optimized through different means. Sometimes, multiple countries must act at the same time; at other times, individual countries' efforts can result in essential regional public goods (e.g., vaccinating border communities and migrant workers) that break the cross-border chain of disease transmission. To reduce health vulnerabilities and strengthen health security, the ASEAN Comprehensive Recovery Framework supports vaccine rollout, ASEAN's disease surveillance system, and ASEAN's Public Health Emergencies and Emerging Diseases. Figure 4 illustrates national and regional vaccination actions and how they reinforce each other.

Figure 4: Linking National Vaccine Programs to Regional Actions

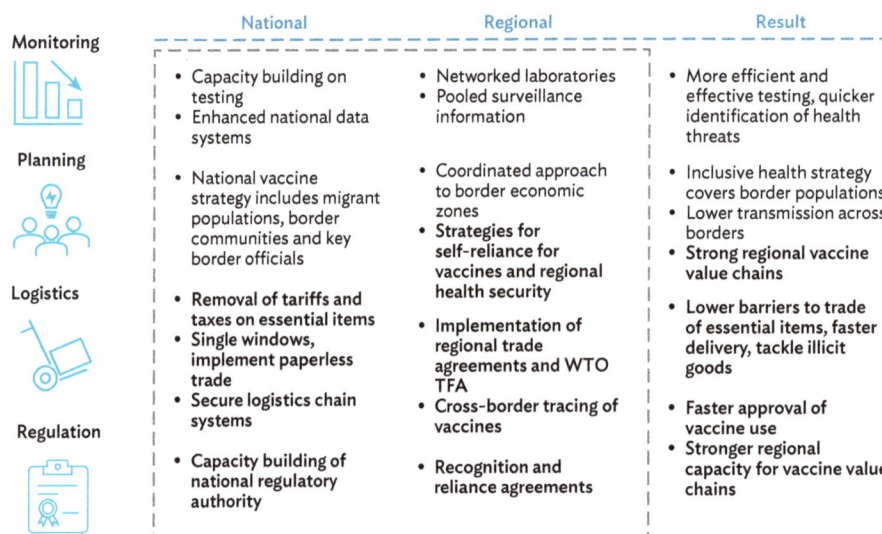

	National	Regional	Result
Monitoring	• Capacity building on testing • Enhanced national data systems	• Networked laboratories • Pooled surveillance information	• More efficient and effective testing, quicker identification of health threats
Planning	• National vaccine strategy includes migrant populations, border communities and key border officials	• Coordinated approach to border economic zones • Strategies for self-reliance for vaccines and regional health security	• Inclusive health strategy covers border populations • Lower transmission across borders • Strong regional vaccine value chains
Logistics	• Removal of tariffs and taxes on essential items • Single windows, implement paperless trade • Secure logistics chain systems	• Implementation of regional trade agreements and WTO TFA • Cross-border tracing of vaccines	• Lower barriers to trade of essential items, faster delivery, tackle illicit goods
Regulation	• Capacity building of national regulatory authority	• Recognition and reliance agreements	• Faster approval of vaccine use • Stronger regional capacity for vaccine value chains

WTO TFA = World Trade Organization Trade Facilitation Agreement.
Source: Asian Development Bank.

Cross-Border Collective Action for Recovery

Intercountry cooperation helps ensure coherence across recovery strategies that support seamless connectivity, the competitiveness of the regional tradable sector, and the cost-effective and mutually beneficial provision of regional public goods. In the last half of 2020, the region and its development partners started planning when and how to restore economic, social, and environmental development and resume progress in achieving the Sustainable Development Goals. Three key dimensions emerged: build better, build differently, and build together.[6] Engaging private sector players for the entire rebuilding effort is crucial to ensure resilience and inclusion and to leverage on their financial and human resources. MDB assistance can help private sector endeavors in infrastructure, financial institutions, supply chains, and trade finance and facilitation (Box 7).

CAREC, GMS, SASEC, and PIF/CROP have proven to be effective platforms for RCI and collective action to foster post–COVID-19 recovery. Tables 4–7 summarize notable RCI and collective action initiatives and MDBs' associated roles and opportunities.

Central Asia Regional Economic Cooperation Program. Supported by MDBs, CAREC countries are using COVID-19 recovery efforts to strengthen development partnerships.

---

[6]   **Build better:** Make the right investments, introduce innovation, and minimize the economic costs of ensuring green, digital, and resilient recovery. **Build differently:** Build high-quality, innovative infrastructure and logistics needed to minimize health risks linked to connectivity and cross-border mobility of people and animals. Improve urban infrastructure to lessen the risk of disease outbreaks. Prioritize regional health security while combating climate change and protecting the environment. **Build together:** Implement trade agreements among economies of Asia and the Pacific to support fair and inclusive trade, create more and better jobs, and foster common standards for workplace conditions and practices. Build resilience in agriculture and operations of SMEs.

Box 7: Paperless Trade: Legislative Reform to Enable Electronic Transferable Records in Asia

A major roadblock to the greater use of paperless trade solutions is the lack of legal recognition of electronic transferable records. After the coronavirus disease (COVID-19) era, the single greatest driver of adoption of electronic records will be their legal recognition by countries. A solution is the Model Law on Electronic Transferable Records, developed by the United Nations Commission on International Trade Law. Only three jurisdictions, however, have adopted it.

The International Chamber of Commerce (ICC), Enterprise Singapore, and the Asian Development Bank (ADB) launched the ICC Digital Standards Initiative in 2020. It focuses on establishing a globally harmonized, digitized trade environment and envisions digital standards that enable seamless digital trade throughout the trade ecosystem, with end-to-end interoperability for exporters, shippers, ports and customs authorities, logistics providers, financiers, and importers. The initiative will strengthen resilience in trade finance and supply chain processes, increase productivity, introduce services at scale, and advance the Sustainable Development Goals. It will leverage technology to reduce the global trade finance gap, particularly among micro, small, and medium-sized enterprises.

Source: ICC and ADB.

Table 4: Central Asia Regional Economic Cooperation Program—
"Build Better" COVID-19 Recovery

Subregion-Led Initiatives	Multilateral Development Bank Roles and Assistance				
	Convenor, Secretariat, Dialogue Partner	Technical Advisor	Financier	Capacity Developer	Knowledge Provider
Building Stronger CAREC Program Development Partnerships	1st Development Partners' Forum on 2 December 2020 Intercountry technical forums (e.g., CAREC Customs Cooperation Committee, Regional Trade Group) Formulation of CAREC Health Strategy 2030 and CAREC Digital Strategy, for ministers' endorsement	MDB and IMF support for high-level policy dialogue on economic and financial stability in CAREC region 2nd Capital Market Development Forum Support country accession to WTO. Advise on implementation of international agreements.	A new regional infrastructure-enabling facility to prepare and cofinance regional infrastructure projects CAREC investments for regional connectivity and customs modernization Disaster risk transfer facility for the CAREC region	Implement the CAREC Gender Strategy 2030. TA to support CAREC countries to apply digital technologies with strengthened ICT capacities; prepare forums new more digital "normal" Introduce a "layered" approach to disaster risk financing combining national and regional solutions.	Support CAREC knowledge-sharing activities with other regions and subregions. CAREC Regional Food Safety Network knowledge platform Introduce a "layered" approach to disaster risk financing combining national and regional solutions.

CAREC = Central Asia Regional Economic Cooperation, GMS = Greater Mekong Subregion, ICT = information and communication technology, IMF = International Monetary Fund, MDB = multilateral development bank, TA = technical assistance, WTO = World Trade Organization.
Source: Asian Development Bank.

Recent and planned efforts include the establishment of the Development Partners' Forum, new sector and thematic subregional strategies, innovative regional infrastructure and disaster risk financing facilities, and new knowledge initiatives. They will use the full suite of MDB capabilities and resources (Table 4).

Greater Mekong Subregion Program. GMS countries have formulated a comprehensive medium-term recovery plan that includes measures to strengthen the subregion's readiness to manage crises. The plan adopts new digital technologies, strengthens trade facilitation and supply chains to bolster regional health security, stresses inclusive economic opportunities, and gives the private sector a bigger role in economic growth. MDBs partnering with GMS can find excellent opportunities to apply their capabilities and resources to subregional recovery (Table 5).

South Asia Subregional Economic Cooperation Program. South Asian countries will embark on post–COVID-19 recovery that stresses strengthened, strategic collective action for RCI governance, planning, and project prioritization. More upstream subregional knowledge work, knowledge sharing, and capacity development, assisted by development partners, including MDBs, will support SASEC sector policy dialogue. MDBs will have more opportunities to support innovative regional market development through transport corridors, trade facilitation, and cross-border energy trade (Table 6).

Table 5: Greater Mekong Subregion—"Build Better" COVID-19 Recovery

Subregion-Led Initiatives	Multilateral Development Bank Roles and Assistance				
	Convenor, Secretariat, Dialogue Partner	Technical Advisor	Financier	Capacity Developer	Knowledge Provider
GMS COVID-19 Response and Recovery Plan 2021–2023	Coordinate on issues requiring greater RCI to effectively respond to COVID-19, build recovery, and prepare for further crises.	Advise on improved migration planning and worker empowerment in preparation for return to work.

Advise on digital technology demonstrations on green and COVID-19–responsive agribusiness supply chains. | Invest in infrastructure at border points, in health facilities for sanitation and hygiene, in testing, and in isolation and quarantine facilities to facilitate the safe movement of people. Invest in digital technologies that link health information across borders. | Build capacity in the regulation of vaccines, supply chain assessment and upgrading, and development or risk communication and vaccine delivery strategies.

Support the plan's One Health, subsector and multisector approaches linking animal health and human health, and work with the transport and tourism sectors. | Strengthen resilience and strategies for trade facilitation, focusing on regional supply chains.

Prepare knowledge products on inter-subregional cooperation on RCI and mobilization of private sector investments in COVID-19–response agribusiness in GMS. |

COVID-19 = coronavirus disease, GMS = Greater Mekong Subregion, RCI = regional cooperation and integration.
Source: Asian Development Bank.

**Table 6: South Asia Subregional Economic Cooperation Program—
"Build Better" COVID-19 Recovery**

Subregion-Led Initiatives	Multilateral Development Bank Roles and Assistance				
	Convenor, Secretariat, Dialogue Partner	Technical Advisor	Financier	Capacity Developer	Knowledge Provider
The Draft Action Plan of South Asia Subregional Economic Cooperation (SASEC) Initiatives 2021–2023 (APSI)	Enhanced national and subregional SASEC institutions, SASEC nodal and senior officials, and working groups and subregions official and working groups and subregions	Strengthened role of the APSI in setting the priorities for planning and accelerated implementation of regional initiatives	The APSI summarizes the status of ongoing SASEC initiatives and proposed priority projects (e.g., transport corridors, trade facilitation, integrated energy markets), which include those for financing by the participating governments and partners.	Enhanced capacity of member countries in planning, implementing, and monitoring SASEC initiatives	Knowledge (e.g., studies and policy papers and briefs), capacity building, and sharing and learning events will all serve as inputs to the various sector working groups and subgroups and SASEC nodal and senior officials' meeting.

Source: Asian Development Bank.

Pacific Islands Forum and Council of Regional Organisations of the Pacific.
Across the Pacific, the recovery of tourism is crucial for rapid, labor-intensive, and environmentally sustainable growth. While each country has unique tourism assets, products, and services, regional approaches can generate significant and shared benefits. A regional perspective would benefit market development, competitiveness, adoption of new technologies and business operation and performance standards, environmental protection and resilience to disasters triggered by natural hazards, and human resource development. MDBs are uniquely placed to help design and implement multicountry and multisector approaches to achieve objectives, using a combination of sovereign, public–private partnership, and private sector initiatives (Table 7).

Table 7: Pacific Community—"Build Better" COVID-19 Recovery

Subregion-Led Initiatives	Multilateral Development Bank Roles and Assistance				
	Convenor, Secretariat, Dialogue Partner	Technical Advisor	Financier	Capacity Developer	Knowledge Provider
The Pacific Tourism Organization COVID-19 Recovery and Strategy	MDBs could engage the organization and individual countries on regional elements of the recovery strategy; e.g., to reduce costs, enhance ease of doing business, improve regional standards and practice, and strengthen compliance.	Support economic and technical planning to inform recovery options and enable more effective transition to changing post–COVID-19 tourism demands, and to guide sound investments.	MDBs' response in the Pacific could include planning and investing in green and safe transport connectivity, particularly green ports and maritime connectivity, and higher-quality waste management.	Support skills recovery and modernization to operate regional travel "bubbles" and adopt digital technologies to widen and deepen regional and global market access.	Support business research and market intelligence for diversification of markets, products and services. Share information regionally on digital transformation of the tourism sector and approaches to innovating tourism governance and partnerships.

COVID-19 = coronavirus disease, MDB = multilateral development bank.
Source: Asian Development Bank.

Case Study: Subregional Collective Actions Up Close—The Greater Mekong Subregion Experience

Background and development context. When it struck, COVID-19 threatened GMS with the risk of significantly reduced growth, incomes, and employment, and the reversal of hard-won progress in poverty reduction. As COVID-19 spread across GMS in early 2020, GMS governments locked down their borders and mitigated transmission. Although GMS economies are different and at different stages of development, they all suffered reduced global demand for goods and services, disrupted regional and global supply chains, and constrained transport of goods across borders.

Balanced multisector response to the COVID-19 emergency. The GMS cross-border response to the COVID-19 emergency involved multiple sectors working in tandem. Drawing upon its recently approved *Health Cooperation Strategy 2019–2023* (ADB 2019) (Figure 5), GMS mobilized national and subregional health communities to help procure diagnostic and laboratory equipment, engage in regional policy dialogue to tackle common capacity constraints, and strengthen surveillance and outbreak responses. Infrastructure providers delivered water, sanitation, and hygiene services, and reused public spaces and modified public transport to meet changing travel needs and conform with public, commercial, and industrial safety protocols. Countries continued implementing the GMS Cross-Border Transport Facilitation Agreement and facilitating trade to ease customs and sanitary and phytosanitary operations. Ongoing projects under the GMS Working Group on Agriculture ensured harmonization of food safety and quality standards, support for rural livelihoods and job creation, control of transboundary animal diseases, and access to green agribusiness supply chains. The GMS Working Group on Environment identified post-pandemic focal areas: green, climate-smart, resilient, and pro-poor operations; sustainable waste management; and biodiversity and wildlife management.

continued on next page

continued

Figure 5: Greater Mekong Subregion Health Cooperation Strategic Framework

STRATEGIC PILLARS			
Pillar 1: Health security as a regional public good	Pillar 2: Health impacts of connectivity and mobility	Pillar 3: Health workforce development	
PROGRAMMING AREAS			CROSSCUTTING
1.1 : Core IHR capacities of national health systems	2.1: Border-area health systems strengthening	3.1: Regional health cooperation leadership	Policy convergence
1.2: One Health response to public health threats	2.2: UHC for migrant and mobile populations	3.2: Intraregional capacity building	Gender mainstreaming
1.3: Cross-border and subregional cooperation on health security	2.3: Health impact assessment of GMS urban and transport infrastructure development		Inclusive and equitable development
ENABLERS			
Synergies between regional platforms and programs	Stakeholder engagement	Research and knowledge products	Information and communication technology	Cross-sector cooperation and coordination

GMS = Greater Mekong Subregion, IHR = International Health Regulations (2005), UHC = universal health coverage.
Source: GMS Working Group on Health Cooperation.

Planning and initiating the recovery. The GMS Leaders' Summit, held on 9 September 2021, endorsed the GMS COVID-19 Response and Recovery Plan 2021–2023 (ADB 2021b) (Figure 6) and the GMS Long-Term Strategic Framework 2030 (GMS-2030) (ADB 2021c) (Figure 7). The three strategic pillars of the response and recovery plan support balanced efforts across GMS countries to (i) resolve issues that require greater RCI to respond to the COVID-19 pandemic, (ii) supplement national COVID-19 responses, and (iii) start implementing GMS-2030. The response and recovery plan lists priority regional investment projects to help execute GMS-2030, offering development partners, including MDBs, diverse opportunities.

Figure 6: Greater Mekong Subregion COVID-19 Response and Recovery Plan 2021–2023

Endorsed by Leaders

The GMS COVID-19 Plan Responds to GMS Countries' Immediate Needs to Mitigate the Impact of the Pandemic.

- It will supplement the GMS-2030, and has three strategic pillars:
  - **A "One Health" approach:** healthy people, animals, crops, food products, and cities.
  - **Protecting the vulnerable and poor**, and safe and orderly labor movement and management
  - **Keeping borders open and accelerating economic recovery.**
- A COVID-19 Response Plan 2021–2023 prepared to respond to the medium-term health, economic, and social impacts of the pandemic and to complement GMS-2030.

COVID-19 = coronavirus disease, GMS = Greater Mekong Subregion.
Source: Asian Development Bank.

continued on next page

continued

Going forward with the GMS Program Long-Term Strategic Framework 2022–2030. During post–COVID-19 recovery, GMS-2030 will apply a multisector and thematic response and short-, medium-, and long-term operational programming. While recognizing the need to reinforce specific pre-pandemic trends, GMS-2030 will consider potential new areas: macroeconomic coordination, digitalization and e-commerce, logistics, labor mobility and safe migration, and special economic zones. The planned interventions will involve broader cross-border collaboration among diverse GMS stakeholders and establish platforms for cross-border collective action.

Figure 7: Greater Mekong Subregion Long-Term Strategic Framework 2022–2030

GMS-2030: New Elements

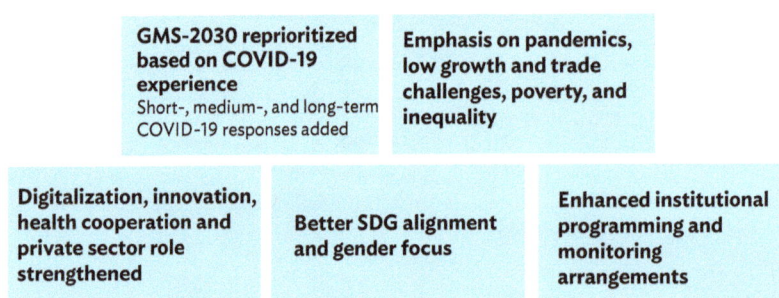

GMS-2030 reprioritized based on COVID-19 experience
Short-, medium-, and long-term COVID-19 responses added

Emphasis on pandemics, low growth and trade challenges, poverty, and inequality

Digitalization, innovation, health cooperation and private sector role strengthened

Better SDG alignment and gender focus

Enhanced institutional programming and monitoring arrangements

COVID-19 = coronavirus disease, GMS = Greater Mekong Subregion, SDG = Sustainable Development Goal.
Source: Asian Development Bank.

Key Lessons

A regional and subregional focus is crucial to manage health emergencies and pandemics. The gap between national and global coordination and action to deal with emerging novel health emergencies is often broad, and links can be tenuous and unworkable and cannot be leveraged in the near term. Regional coordination and cooperation are an essential, workable, and proven strategy to achieve timely, coordinated, and cohesive responses to regional health crises and to create and apply innovations.

Regional and subregional platforms acted inclusively, linked national and regional agendas, and garnered assistance from MDBs and other development partners. Effective multicountry coordination and MDB cooperation to manage the pandemic were possible because well-established RCI subregional platforms linked policy decisions and programs across neighboring countries. Subregional platforms provided venues to engage development partners, including MDBs, and to mobilize diverse advisory, technical, and financial support.

All stakeholders should take collective action quickly and flexibly, and jointly shift timeframes inward, reprioritize operations, and adapt business processes and resource allocation. RCI subregional platforms take open, pragmatic, and flexible approaches to cross-border cooperation. They benefit from their experience in responding to regional public health crises and using existing coordination platforms, specifically in the health sector.

Countries should seek opportunities to apply common standards and to broaden and strengthen subregional and even region-wide capabilities. For example, RCI subregional programs and their MDB and development partners adeptly promoted common standards for sustaining cross-border flows, such as customs security protocols, deployment of technical personnel, immigration, and equipment and supply clearances.

New RCI opportunities have emerged to support post–COVID-19 recovery.
To maximize the potential gains from large regional and multilateral trade agreements, Asia and the Pacific need to upgrade regional connectivity infrastructure and trade logistics, reduce trade costs through greater digitalization, and resolve behind-the-border bottlenecks such as restrictive regulations.

The region is signaling new roles for RCI collective action, supported by multilateral development partners. Multilateral assistance can help countries develop platforms for cross-border project design and delivery. Such assistance can provide ancillary support for regional capacity building to bridge critical skill and competency gaps that undermine cross-border programs and projects.

MDBs can work more closely together. They can use RCI subregional platforms as a framework for constructive dialogue among themselves to ensure that, by working together, they make the best use of their collective resources in complementary ways to support and benefit participating countries.

The Way Forward

Building on successes and accomplishments in 2020 and 2021—quickly, wisely, effectively, and together—countries must continue to act collectively to prevail over the pandemic and achieve full post–COVID-19 recovery.

Reaching the Sustainable Development Goals requires even greater RCI to help countries face core policy challenges, such as providing mutually beneficial inclusive and sustainable growth, maintaining national and cross-border security, ensuring environmental sustainability, and developing regional perspectives and a more robust Asian voice in the global community.

Asia and the Pacific's RCI subregional programs will continue to be indispensable platforms through which the region prepares for and responds to crises and implements multicountry programs to build back better. Using innovative coordination and cooperation approaches, the subregional platforms must implement new sector and thematic strategies and investment frameworks suitable to the new normal. Doing so will entail extending and evolving RCI to deliver broader and more diverse socioeconomic and environmental benefits across countries and stakeholders.

The region's development partners, including MDBs, have contributed significantly to ending the emergency and starting the recovery. However, further innovations in knowledge work, technical and advisory services, programming of operations, and resource mobilization and allocation will be essential.

References

Asian Development Bank (ADB). 2018. Investing in Health Security for Sustainable Development in Asia and the Pacific: Managing Health Threats through Regional and Intersectoral Cooperation. *ADB Sustainable Development Working Paper Series*. Manila.

———. 2019. *Health Cooperation Strategy 2019–2023*. Manila.

———. 2021a. *Asian Economic Integration Report 2021: Making Digital Platforms Work for Asia and the Pacific.* Manila.

———. 2021b. *Greater Mekong Subregion Covid-19 Response and Recovery Plan 2021–2023*. Manila.

———. 2021c. *Greater Mekong Subregion Program Long-Term Strategic Framework 2030*. Second draft. Phnom Penh.

3 Quality Regional Connectivity

Highlights

- Global trade is facing trade tensions, pandemic-related shocks, environmental and climate changes, and technology shifts. While trade, infrastructure, and connectivity remained resilient throughout the pandemic and are supporting global recovery, long-term challenges remain.

- "Building back better" can secure short- and long-term benefits and is critical to facing challenges.

- Quality connectivity infrastructure remains imperative to trade. Information and communication technology infrastructure will become as important as ports and roads, and developing economies need to prepare urgently for a future where automation and digital connectivity are the basis of competitiveness.

- Global trade needs to transition to a net zero carbon economy within a few decades. Doing so requires the greening of all production and connectivity infrastructure to ensure the sustainability of trade and prosperity. National policy makers, multilateral development banks, and the private sector must come together to secure the transition.

The post–COVID-19 recovery presents a great opportunity to strengthen resilience and sustainability together and holistically. Infrastructure must connect more economies and citizens and be a key part of climate change mitigation and net zero transition. The prize will be a greener, more resilient, and more inclusive system of trade as development pathways toward shared global prosperity.

Introduction

The global trade system is undergoing a series of well-documented shocks. It faces deeper challenges, some accentuated by the coronavirus disease (COVID-19) pandemic. As countries emerge from the crisis, investment in quality infrastructure will present a key opportunity to realize triple benefits: a short-term economic boost, long-term growth and jobs, and accelerated transition to a net zero carbon economy. Although trade tensions between the United States (US) and the People's Republic of China (PRC) are often in the headlines, trade restrictions by various economies have been rising. Pandemic-related restrictions—affecting critical supplies, personal protective equipment, or vaccines—are lingering concerns for policy makers. Vaccine production and distribution, for example, underscore the potential for trade disputes. Supply chain bottlenecks continued to be felt. Competition for critical industrial resources could also add to trade tensions.

Technological progress—such as digitalization, automation, and artificial intelligence—has begun to change the nature of connectivity and trade. Greater automation and its potential to allow onshoring could displace some trade. Developing economies can no longer attract foreign investments based solely on low-cost labor. Digital infrastructure and the connectivity it brings are critical to trade, much like ports and roads. Yet, the pandemic has exposed the large information and communication technology (ICT) and digital-readiness divide between and within economies. Developing economies will have to catch up or risk being left further behind.

The signing of the Regional Comprehensive Economic Partnership (RCEP) forms the largest free trade area by gross domestic product (GDP), spanning high-, middle-, and low-income economies. RCEP marks the first time that the three large manufacturing hubs in Asia (the PRC, Japan, and the Republic of Korea) have come together under such an agreement. Increasingly, trade is about services and information, and regulation and standards, which require more encompassing agreements such as the Comprehensive and Progressive Agreement for Trans-Pacific Partnership.

Equipment check. The Institutional Strengthening of the Nauru Utilities Corporation project supports the organization's management and governance (photo by Eric Sales/ADB).

The agreements are highly conducive to increasing regional sourcing and production sharing and show that countries are willing to cooperate for the common good. Goodwill is critical to building quality regional connectivity to meet major challenges. Greenhouse gas (GHG) emissions of global trade will become an existential and complex issue. Trade relies on movements of components and final products between distant locations, with implications for the climate and local environments. Production has major environmental impacts. The sustainability of trade requires the greening of production, transport, and logistics everywhere.

Trade and Connectivity Resilient through the Pandemic but Challenges Remain

The onset of the pandemic was a major stress test for businesses, infrastructure, and the global trade system, including the functioning of global value chains (GVCs). In April 2020, the World Trade Organization (WTO) projected that global trade would contract by as much as 32% in 2020. The volume of international merchandise trade had fallen precipitously by about 15% (Figure 8).

However, trade flows recovered fast despite on-and-off resurgence of the virus. By the end of 2020, global trade volume had exceeded pre-pandemic levels, having increased 1.2% year-on-year (5.8% in value terms). Shipping lines, ports, air cargo, rail, and other logistics and trade infrastructure came under severe strain during the pandemic. First were the lockdowns, stoppages at facilities, and workers on quarantine, which crippled operations. Then came the release of pent-up demand after the easing of lockdowns in mid-2020, including the effects of government stimulus, shifts in consumer spending from services to goods, and business restocking,[7] leading to a surge in demand for manufactures from Asia and, with it, for transport. Volatility amid continuing intermittent capacity closures has led to historically high imbalances and bottlenecks in multiple parts of the system.

Figure 8: Volume of World Merchandise Trade

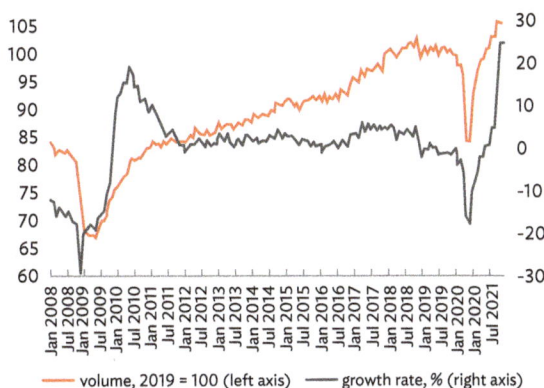

— volume, 2019 = 100 (left axis)   — growth rate, % (right axis)

Source: CPB World Trade Monitor.

Figure 9: Global Trade Carrying Capacity

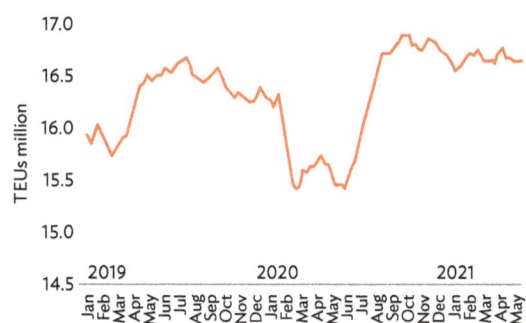

Source: World Bank (2021).

---

7   According to the US Census Bureau, e-commerce sales in the US grew by more than 30% in 2020.

Policy makers consider logistics a key sector or essential service and exempted them from some restrictions, stepped up interagency coordination, or simplified custom processes, particularly for essential and emergency goods. Many players accelerated the adoption of digital technologies (UNCTAD 2020b). Logistics operators adapted to the situation. Airlines, for example, converted passenger planes into cargo operations. Collectively, the measures have kept trade flowing.

While bottlenecks and transport stresses are still evident in the recovery period, the maritime and port sector has on the whole proved resilient. Deployed container-ship capacity began to recover in May 2020 and exceeded pre-pandemic levels by mid-summer 2020 (Figure 9). Despite operational constraints, vessels' turnaround times at ports did not seem to have increased significantly (World Bank 2021a). By the fourth quarter of 2020, global port turnover exceeded previous years' levels (Figure 10). A large part of the connectivity network remained intact. The average number of port-to-port connections (as measured by the number of origin–destination pairs in shipping networks) had declined by less than 10% by May 2020 compared with 2019 levels (World Bank 2021).

The developments highlight the importance of hard and soft infrastructure coming together to adapt to shocks and disruptions. Although shipping costs remain elevated in 2021 (Figure 11), global trade has continued largely smoothly, underpinning economic recovery. The composite global connected index—covering trade, information, people, capital—has shown resilience and broad-based recovery since the last half of 2020, with many Asian economies powering the charge (DHL 2020).

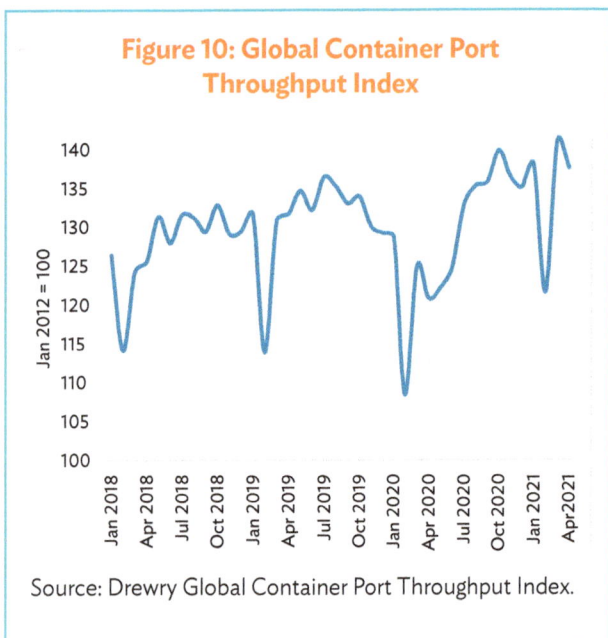

Figure 10: Global Container Port Throughput Index

Source: Drewry Global Container Port Throughput Index.

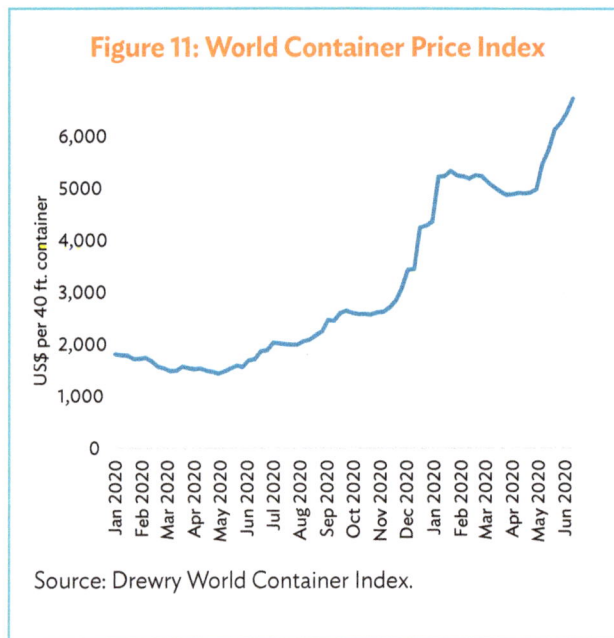

Figure 11: World Container Price Index

Source: Drewry World Container Index.

Quality Infrastructure for Trade and Supply Chains

The rise of GVCs has been a feature of global trade since the 1990s. The fragmentation of production into parts and intermediates to be produced in various locations has allowed firms to reap great economies of scale and developing economies to enter global production, the benefits of which are well documented (World Bank 2020). The quality of power, logistics, and transport infrastructure greatly determines whether geographic dispersion is economically feasible: quality infrastructure underpins global production sharing and trade.

Raising Overall Level and Quality of Infrastructure

Not surprisingly, countries' cross-sectional data show a clear correlation between infrastructure quality and GVC participation (Figure 12). GVC participation seems to take off when countries achieve a certain standard of infrastructure quality (3 to 4 on the X-axis). The relationship is expected to be mutually reinforcing: infrastructure improvements are likely to induce firms to participate more in GVCs by alleviating key structural bottlenecks, and GVC participation might allow infrastructure investments to be economically productive.

Figure 12: Binscatter Correlation between Infrastructure Quality and Global Value Chain Participation across Countries

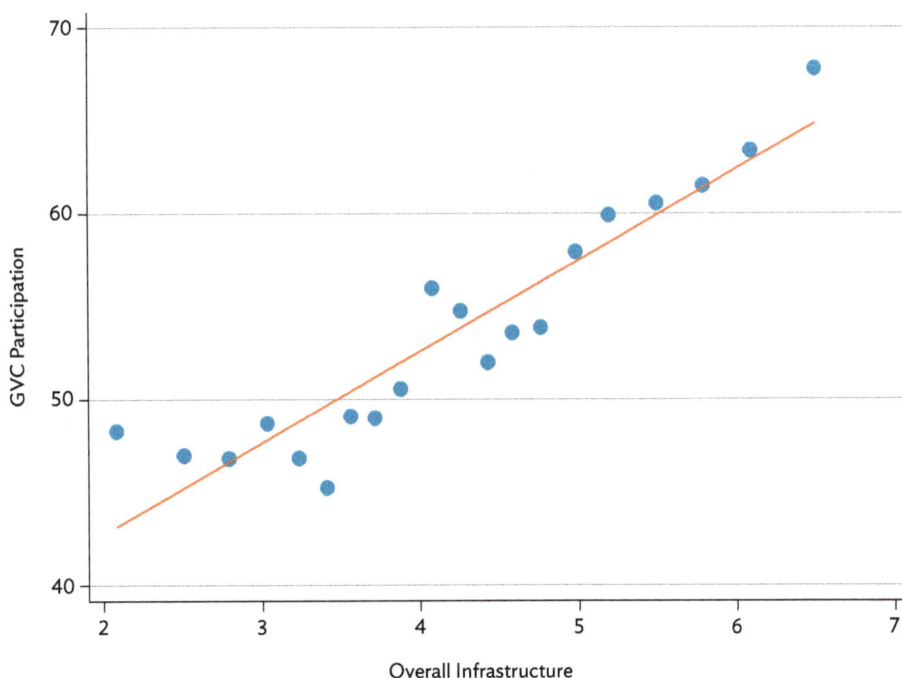

GVC = global value chain.

Note: The X-axis reflects the infrastructure scores of economies (World Economic Forum [WEF]), while the Y-axis reflects the level of GVC participation computed from the Eora dataset. The binscatter correlation groups the samples into bins, enhancing the visualization of large datasets.

Source: Eora database, WEF, and Asian Infrastructure Investment Bank calculations.

Digging deeper, the importance of various infrastructure types becomes evident, as shown in Figure 13. Electricity is key, as poor-quality power disrupts production and raises costs, affecting the whole value chain. Unsurprisingly, an extremely strong positive association exists between the quality of power and GVC participation (Figure 13b). Power outages reduce export participation based on evidence from a large sample of firms in the World Bank Enterprise Survey database.

Figure 13: Binscatter Correlation between Global Value Chain Participation and Various Infrastructure Quality Measures

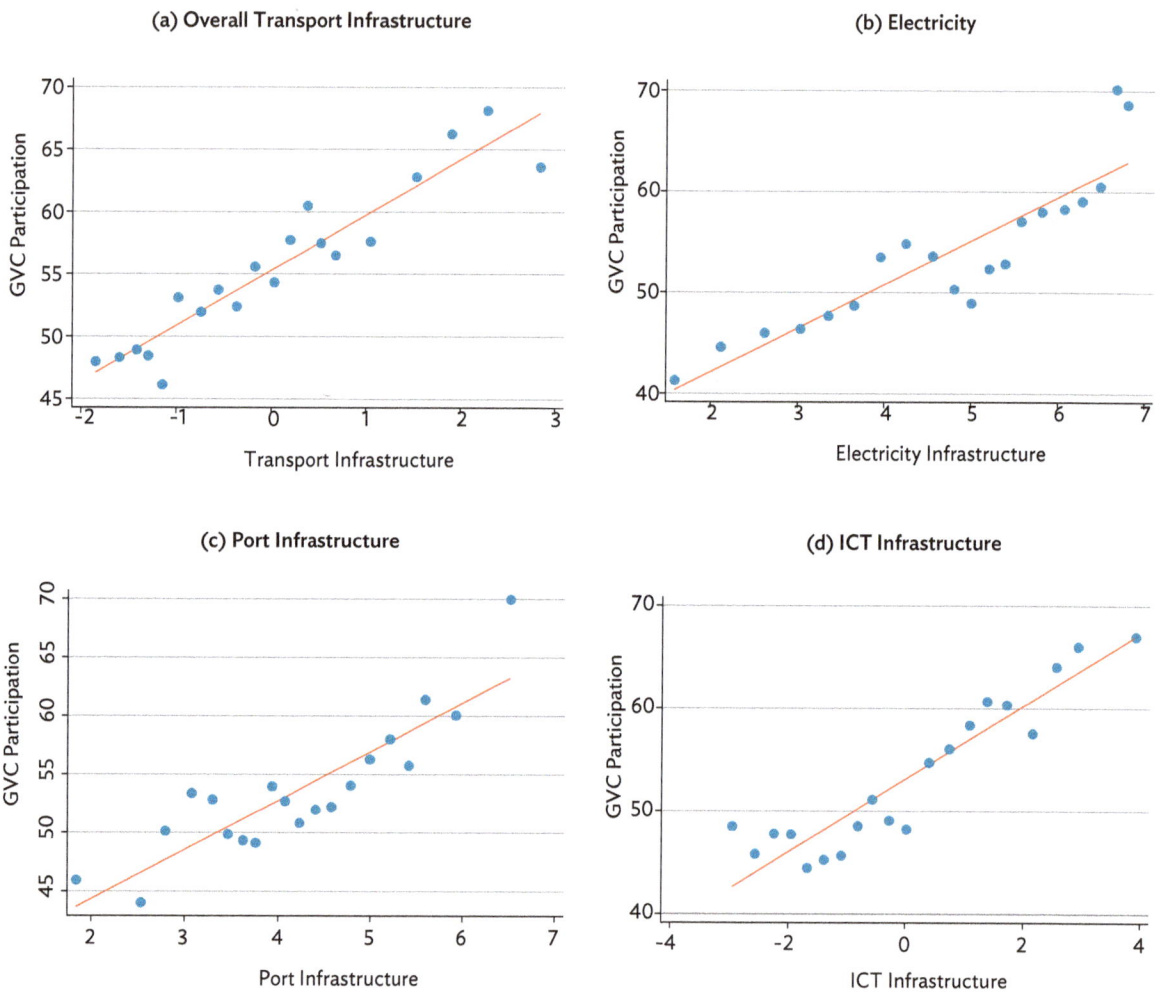

GVC = global value chain, ICT = information and communication technology.

Note: The transport infrastructure index is computed based on the first principal component of the quality of roads and railways, while the ICT infrastructure index is calculated using the first principal component of per capita broadband subscribers, per capita fixed telephone lines, international internet bandwidth, per capita mobile broadband subscribers, per capita mobile telephone subscribers, and percentage of the population using the internet.

Source: Eora database, World Economic Forum, and Asian Infrastructure Investment Bank calculations.

Weak transport infrastructure or bureaucracy, leading to time or cost overruns, inhibits a country's participation in GVCs (Lanz and Piermartini 2018). The close linkage between quality of transport infrastructure and GVC participation is evident from Figure 13a. With nearly 70% of value carried by maritime transport, port infrastructure and customs procedures influence a country's GVC participation (Bottasso et al. 2018). High dwell time at ports introduces uncertainties in supply of goods, greatly impeding GVC exports as the manufacturing supply chain is tightly controlled with just-in-time inventory systems.

Evidence is emerging that the quality of transport connectivity is critical for high-technology industries. Using the country-by-country trade flow matrix, the trade centrality of an economy can be computed.[8] An economy with large trade flow in a sector, and which is well-connected to other important nodes, will be deemed more central. For less complex goods, no obvious correlation exists between the centrality of economies and the quality of their transport infrastructure. But for complex products, a much higher correlation exists between trade centrality and transport infrastructure (Figure 14), highlighting the criticality of transport infrastructure for economies upgrading to more complex products.

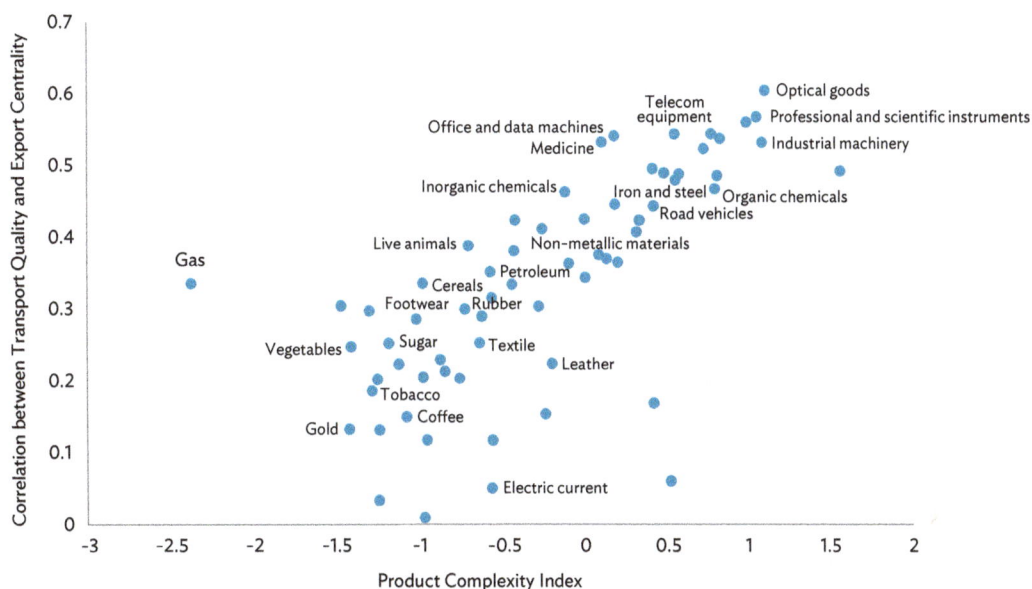

Figure 14: Export Product Complexity and Correlation between Transport Infrastructure and Centrality

Note: For each product, the cross-country centrality scores (based on eigenvector centrality) are computed and correlated with transport infrastructure quality. The figure presents the summary of the underlying correlations (between centrality scores and infrastructure quality for all the sectors), across products of various complexity.

Data sources: World Economic Forum Transport Quality index, Atlas of Economic Complexity Product Complexity Index and Asian Infrastructure Investment Bank staff calculations of product-level trade centrality.

---

[8] This refers to the eigenvector measure of centrality, capturing the influence of a node in a network.

Integrating External and Internal Connectivity Infrastructure

Inland and external-facing infrastructure must be integrated. Poor infrastructure and high transport costs impede participation in GVCs, particularly for downstream industries (Antras and de Gortari 2020). With maritime trade accounting for the bulk of global merchandise trade, seaports are the gateways of trade participation for most firms. Exporting and importing firms will tend to locate close to a seaport to minimize transport costs and time. But closeness does not need to refer to physical distance. Firms can enjoy significantly shorter travel times to a port that is well-connected by a highway network than to one that lacks road connectivity, even if the well-connected port is farther away.

The availability of digital maps, data, geographic information system (GIS) tools, and computing capacity in recent years has greatly improved policy makers' capacity to plan interregional and intermodal connectivity. Take, for example, the port and road nexus. Aided by digital maps, isochrones can be computed for ports; an isochrone is a geometric shape that maps the boundary of how far one can travel from a fixed point in a given amount of time. The greater the number and quality of road connections a port has, the larger its associated isochrones, implying that it has the capacity to serve a larger population and geographic space. For example, Figure 15 shows the geographic cover of the 4-hour isochrone for some Asian ports.

Domestic connectivity can not only boost exports but also alleviate spatial inequalities. In the PRC, for instance, activities used to be heavily concentrated in coastal areas with easy access to various types of transport infrastructure and a better business environment. Areas such as the Pearl and Yangtze river deltas will no doubt remain important, but more noncoastal cities are exporting a much higher share of intermediate goods than 2 decades ago, bringing development to inland regions.

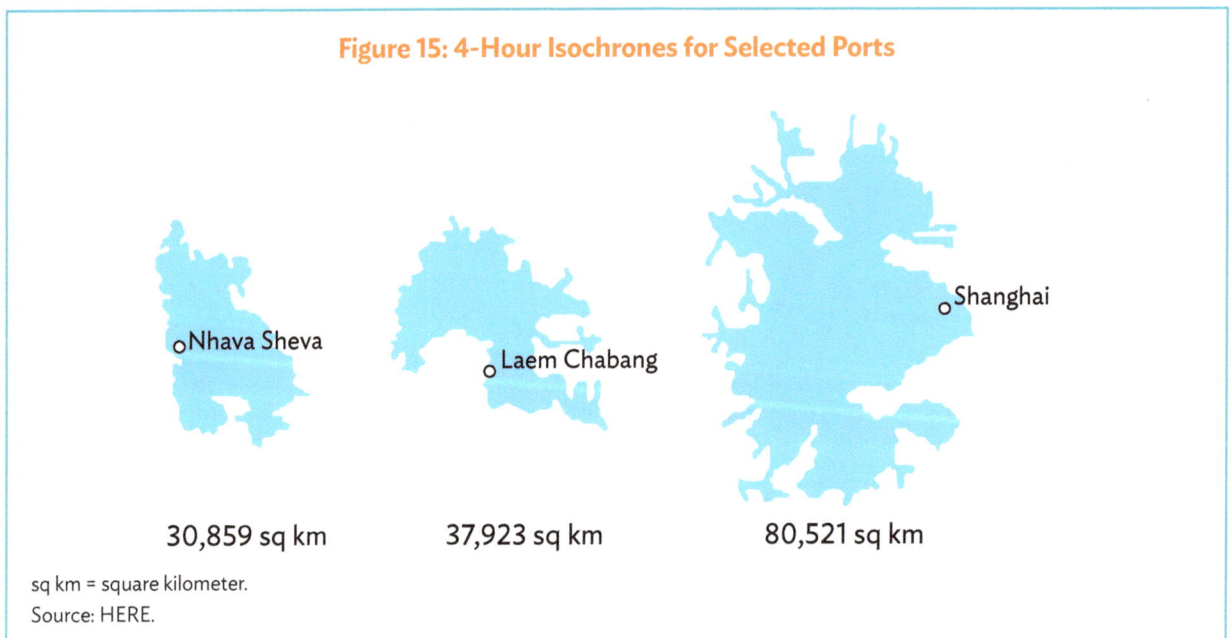

Figure 15: 4-Hour Isochrones for Selected Ports

Nhava Sheva

Laem Chabang

Shanghai

30,859 sq km   37,923 sq km   80,521 sq km

sq km = square kilometer.
Source: HERE.

Rising Importance of Information and Communication Technology

The pandemic has brought home the importance of digital transformation. Advanced robotics, artificial intelligence, cloud computing, the Internet of Things (IoT), data capture and analytics, and digital fabrication are greatly automating and optimizing production, which now affects trade and supply chains (World Bank 2019). Technologies such as digital platforms for e-commerce, digital payments, automated document processing, and IoT reduce coordination and matching costs, making logistics highly efficient. An analysis of more than 9,000 firms in India shows that digital competence helps firms upgrade to more sophisticated product lines that capture higher value-added in GVCs (Banga 2019).

Yet, the COVID-19 pandemic has exposed challenges. The diffusion of digital infrastructure services remains highly uneven. Only half of the global population has access to the internet, with access dropping to less than 30% in parts of South Asia and sub-Saharan Africa. Among members of the Asian Infrastructure Investment Bank, nearly 2.4 billion people do not have access to the internet, most living in India, the PRC, Indonesia, Pakistan, Bangladesh, and the Philippines (Gao 2020). Consequently, many of the countries have difficulty leveraging digital technology to overcome the economic hardships caused by lockdowns and social distancing and to access basic goods and services. Divides exist within countries along regional or social lines. For example, in Bangladesh, 32% of males have access to mobile money accounts compared with 10% of females. Such disparity hampers economic participation and worsens in-country inequalities.

Evidence is emerging that robotics and automation in developed economies can displace jobs in developing economies (Faber 2020). Developing economies must, therefore, prepare for a future where ICT infrastructure becomes as important as roads and ports were in the past, if not more so.

Supportive Trade Policy and Regional Cooperation

GVCs are more regionalized, given the need to reduce trade costs for production sharing (Baldwin and Freeman 2020). The pandemic has given impetus to go for shorter and closer supplies as firms seek to improve supply chain resilience, which needs to be supported via deeper regional cooperation. The signing of RCEP is a key positive development in a difficult year. The agreement recommits various economies to openness and development. It is also an agreement with many breakthroughs.

First, it is the largest free trade zone by GDP size. Second, RCEP further simplifies rules of origin of many existing free trade agreements, expediting the region's progress in becoming a single production base. Third, RCEP comes at a time of rising protectionism and slowdown in GVC participation. Greater multilateral cooperation among countries is particularly necessary when many countries are grappling with the economic fallout from the pandemic. Fourth, RCEP encompasses high-, middle-, and low-income economies, which, in principle, gives rise to the potential of more comparative advantage in trade along different parts of the value chain, allowing countries to specialize in different parts of the value chain but to cohere into a single regional production base. RCEP is expected to offset, for example, the US–PRC trade dispute and add to Asian RCEP members' GDPs (Petri and Plummer 2020).[9]

Despite positive developments, however, such production sharing and trade will not come about automatically. For RCEP to be most effective, infrastructure connectivity must be improved among all members. Infrastructure quality still varies among RCEP members (more so than among members of the European Union or the North American Free Trade Agreement), with some at low levels of infrastructure development. The disparity underscores the importance of promoting infrastructure investment that further strengthens connectivity to reap RCEP's full benefits for all members.

RCEP is just one step on a journey to more connectivity. While ambitious on traditional trade issues such as tariffs and regulations, the agreement does not deal much with trade in services and information flows. Additional agreements are needed to support the development of value chains, especially in digital infrastructure.

Regional cooperation is not just about such trade agreements. Sector cooperation can be important and meaningful. The South Asian Subregional Economic Cooperation (SASEC) Program, for example, has mapped out many connectivity initiatives and was updated in 2019 to bridge gaps in energy and transport networks. Infrastructure investments in each country can be part of a wider regional network, thereby providing greater economic returns to the investments and wider spillover benefits. For instance, Bangladesh's investment in its gas pipelines can be expanded to connect and serve the subregion's countries, increasing network resilience and bringing greater benefits for the whole subregion.

Infrastructure and Net Zero Transition

Preparing for Higher Trade Costs

The discussion on quality connectivity infrastructure must confront a fundamental challenge. International trade incurs carbon footprints, estimated at about 2.1 gigatons per annum, given the need to transport goods (Figure 16). In general, carbon emission is correlated with the weight of goods, distance traveled, and mode of transport. For industry-related goods—most closely linked to GVCs—the distance weight incurred by goods has flatlined in recent years. However, the distance weight of agriculture and oil-related goods continues to rise moderately.

First, the transport of fuels has a high carbon footprint, given the weight and distance traveled. Renewable power generation, to the extent that it reduces fuel imports, reduces carbon emissions. Second, trade policies influence carbon emissions. For example, with the rising trade tensions in 2017/18, distance weight has seen an uptick as trade in agricultural goods is diverted.

---

[9]   The authors show that while RCEP would benefit Asia, gains would be higher with India's entry. The positive impact of RCEP would be heightened in the absence of trade war.

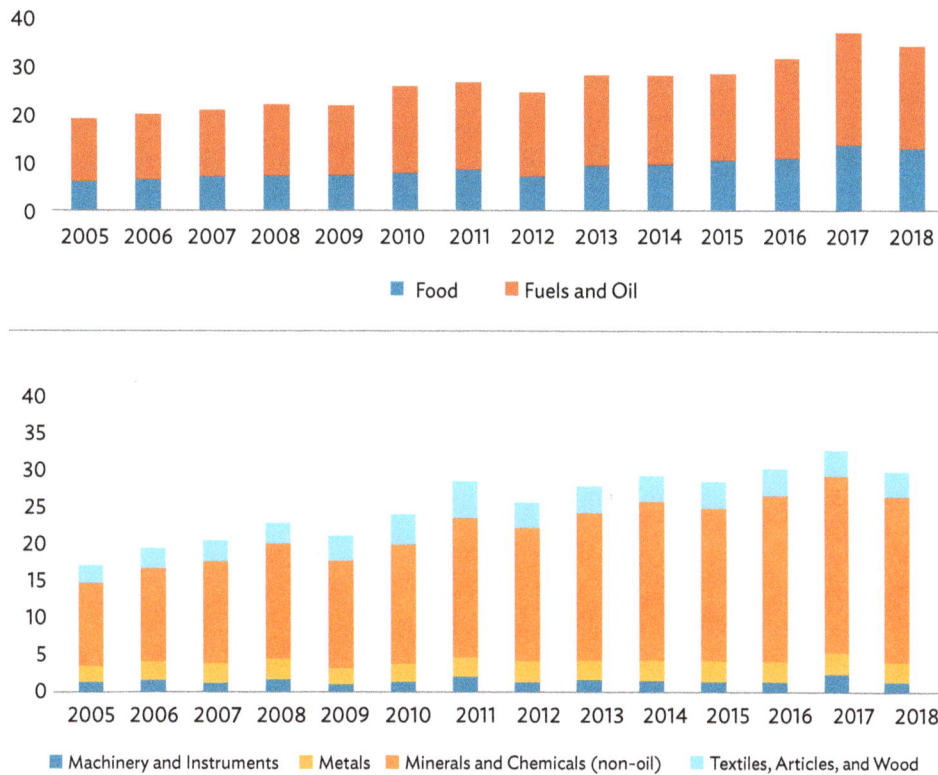

Figure 16: Distance Weight of Internationally Traded Goods
(ton-kilometer)

Source: UN Comtrade and Asian Infrastructure Investment Bank calculations.

Globally, GHG emissions, including from land use, stood at about 49.4 gigatons in 2016. Freight emission (international and domestic) is estimated at about 3.6 gigatons.[10] By 2050, demand for freight and nonurban passenger transport is projected to grow by 225%, with Asia alone projected to account for 56% of the world's surface freight emissions (International Transport Forum 2019).[11] Greener logistics—the effort to minimize the ecological impact of logistical activities—will, therefore, become key to sustainability.

Transport infrastructure must reduce its carbon footprint. Of concern is that carbon pricing of trade logistics would present a bigger challenge for developing economies. Shapiro (2016) comprehensively analyzed the impact of carbon pricing on trade costs and showed that higher trade costs can affect developing economies more negatively, even as the introduction of a

---

[10]   See Our World in Data (2020). About 16.2% of global emissions are, broadly, from transport: roads (11.9%), aviation (1.9%), shipping (1.7%), rail (0.4%), and pipelines (0.3%). Emissions from road transport are estimated to be split about 6:4 between passenger and freight, and from aviation about 8:2. Freight transport accounts for some 4% of GHG emissions and 9% of carbon dioxide emissions (McKinnon 2020).

[11]   Surface freight refers to goods transported by rail, road, and inland waterway.

carbon price improves global welfare by pricing in the externality. Many developing economies export commodities and raw materials (i.e., heavier goods), which require more shipping fuel and, thus, will be impacted by the carbon price. In the longer term, the sector's sustainability will depend on the development and commercialization of low-carbon fuels (International Energy Agency 2020).

Investing in Carbon Reduction Technologies

Europe's pilot CO_2 TransPorts project, launched in late 2019, aims to capture, transport, and store carbon dioxide from the three most important ports in the region—Rotterdam, Antwerp, and the North Sea—with operations starting in 2030 (European Commission 2019). Supported by their governments, the port authorities and national natural gas infrastructure entities of the three jurisdictions will cooperate to develop and operate an open-access carbon capture and storage (CCS) platform.

In phase one, an onshore pipeline will run through the Port of Rotterdam to a compressor station, which will then pump the carbon dioxide into the depleted P18 gas fields off the coast of Rotterdam for storage. In phase two, a network of cross-border carbon dioxide pipelines will connect Antwerp and the North Sea Port with Rotterdam. If phase two is successful, phase three may be opened to additional members.

Further applications of CCS in transport and logistics will help achieve global carbon reduction goals, an example of how regional cooperation can lead to common and viable carbon reduction infrastructure.

Infrastructure to Green All Production and Trade

Exported goods embed significant levels of carbon emissions, which are traded across the border. Gross emissions embedded in exports amount to about 8 gigatons per year, or close to 20% of global emissions, with Organisation for Economic Co-operation and Development (OECD) countries being largely net importers of carbon emissions and non-OECD countries exporters (OECD 2019).

As countries focus on reducing domestic emissions and meeting their national targets under the Paris Agreement, they will increasingly be looking at carbon emissions embedded in trade to prevent carbon leakage. Economies and organizations that plug into GVCs via clean energy will enjoy a competitive advantage. Greening trade and achieving commonly high standards are perhaps the most fundamental and difficult of all challenges and rest on a few fundamental pillars:

- Continuously and quickly scaling up renewable energy in each economy or CCS, where applicable. Clean energy underpins the sustainability of all production and consumption, including goods and services produced for trade.

- Complementing renewable energy production with renewable energy trade. Asia still lags significantly in cross-border transmission of electricity, and more such infrastructure and grid integration are necessary (AIIB 2019). Trade in biofuels and hydrogen can be expected to become more mainstream for longer-distance energy trade (Ernst & Young 2021).

- Recognizing and expediting the shift of some manufacturing to locations with abundant renewable energy or green comparative advantage. For example, industries such as steelmaking, which require a large amount of energy, are now expected to be closer to sources of abundant renewable energy (The Economist 2021). Connectivity and logistics infrastructure can be aligned to meet the expectation.

- Greening transport and logistics.

The pillars must be supported by massive investments to remake infrastructure, from energy generation and transmission to transport systems. The transition requires strong international cooperation, including financing, research and technical assistance, and regulatory support.

Green, Resilient, and Inclusive

The pandemic highlighted many existing fault lines, including trade tensions, infrastructure divides, and supply chain vulnerabilities. The pandemic offers key lessons on the need to prepare for future shocks, including from climate change and technology. The challenges are intertwined. The post–COVID-19 recovery presents a great opportunity to meet them together and holistically. Infrastructure must be a key part of climate change mitigation and net zero transition. Infrastructure must be highly resilient against future shocks and connect more economies and citizens. The prize will be a greener, more resilient, and more inclusive system of trade that can continue to underpin global prosperity and offer development pathways for developing economies.

Keeping trade going. Port of Suva is the maritime gateway to Fiji's capital, Suva (photo by Eric Sales/ADB).

References

Antras, P. and A. de Gortari. 2020. On the Geography of Global Value Chains. *Econometrica.*

Baldwin, R. and R. Freeman. 2020. Supply Chain Contagion Waves: Thinking Ahead on Manufacturing "Contagion and Reinfection" from the COVID Concussion. 1 April.

Banga, K. 2019. Digital Technologies and "Value" Capture in Global Value Chains: Empirical Evidence from Indian Manufacturing Firms. *United Nations University World Institute for Development Economics Research Working Paper.* 2019/43. Helsinki.

Bottasso, A., M. Conti, P. Costacurta de Sa Porto, C. Ferrari, and A. Tei. 2018. Port Infrastructures and Trade: Empirical Evidence from Brazil. *Transportation Research Part A: Policy and Practice.* 107. pp. 126–39.

Cerdeiro, D. A., A. Komaromi, Y. Liu, and M. Saeed. 2020. World Seaborne Trade in Real Time: A Proof of Concept for Building AIS-based Nowcasts from Scratch. *IMF Working Paper.* Washington, DC: International Monetary Fund.

CPB World Trade Monitor. 2021. *CPB World Trade Monitor.* 9 March.

DHL. 2020. DHL Global Connectedness Index 2020.

European Commission. 2019a. *Annex VII: Union List of Projects of Commin Interest section 12.3.* Brussels.

———. 2019b. *Candidate PCI projects in cross-border carbon dioxide transport networks.* Brussels: European Commission.

Faber, M. 2020. Robots and Reshoring: Evidence from Mexican Labor Markets. *Journal of International Economics.* 127.

International Energy Agency. 2020. *International Shipping.* Paris.

International Transport Forum. 2019. *ITF Transport Outlook 2019.* Paris.

Lanz, R. and R. Piermartini. 2018. Specialization Within Global Value Chains: The Role of Additive Transport Costs. *WTO Staff Working Papers.* ERSD-2018-05. Geneva: World Trade Organization.

McKinnon, A. 2020. *Decarbonizing Freight Transport: The Scale of the Challenge.* Hamburg: Kuhne Logistics University.

Petri, P. A. and M. G. Plummer. 2020. East Asia Decouples from United States: Trade War, Covid-19, and East Asia's New Trade Blocs. *Peterson Institute for International Economics Working Paper.* 20-9. Washington, DC.

Shapiro, J. S. 2016. Trade Costs, CO_2, and the Environment. *American Economic Journal: Economic Policy.* 8 (4). pp. 220–54.

United Nations Conference on Trade and Development (UNCTAD). 2020b. How Countries Can Leverage Trade Facilitation to defeat the COVID-19 pandemic. 1 May.

World Bank. 2019. *Technological Innovation, Supply Chain Trade, and Workers in a Globalized World.* Washington, DC.

———. 2020. *World Development Report 2020: Trading for Development in the Age of Global Value Chains.* Washington, DC.

———. 2021. COVID-19 Trade Watch. March 9.

World Trade Organization. 2020a. Trade Set to Plunge as COVID-19 Pandemic Upends Global Economy. 8 April.

———. 2020b. *World Trade Primed for Strong but Uneven Recovery after COVID-19 Pandemic Shock.* March 2021.

———. 2021a. *Services Trade Recovery Not Yet in Sight.* January 2021.

———. 2021b. *Third Quarter 2020 Trade in Services.*

———. 2021c. *Fourth Quarter 2020 Trade in Services.*

4 Inclusive Trade, Investment, and Migration

Cross-border economic integration delivers productivity growth. The overall gains from trade and foreign direct investment can thus be leveraged further by policies that spread the benefits and reduce barriers to the international flow of goods and factors of production. Multilateral development banks can support and coordinate such efforts.

Highlights

Trade, foreign investment, and migration boost productivity by spreading knowledge and new production technologies across borders.

However, the structural transformation expedited by trade, foreign investment, and migration is likely to skew the distribution of income and increase inequality as benefits may accrue to the more highly skilled and those living in richer, urban locations.

Gains from globalization can be used to fund policies that help spread the benefits of international economic integration and strengthen popular support for the cross-border flow of goods, capital, and labor. Such policies could include:

- Reallocation of resources across firms, sectors, and geographic areas can be supported by strengthening social safety nets, promoting retraining and vocational training in cooperation with employers, providing skill certification, and improving job information.

- Targeted benefits may be needed to reduce the cost of economic dislocation in certain sectors and geographical areas.

- The capacity of economies to benefit from trade and foreign investment can be strengthened by fostering linkages between foreign investors and local suppliers of goods and services, helping diffuse information about business opportunities, promoting on-the-job training, and investing in hard infrastructure to enable domestic firms to benefit from knowledge spillover and increased demand for goods and services from foreign firms.

- Investment promotion agencies can play an important role in aligning the profile of foreign investment with the country's skill base and the level of technological development.

- Multilateral development banks (MDBs) can support such efforts by financing investments in infrastructure; coordinating initiatives to reduce barriers to trade and investment, for instance, by streamlining regulations and customs procedures; offering policy advice to help countries develop investment strategies and export-oriented industries that best suit their skill mix; and easing the exchange of best practices across countries.

Introduction

Cross-border trade and investment have been important drivers of economic growth, supporting the structural transformation of economies and leveraging countries' natural resources, labor, and skills. Migration flows benefit home countries (where migrants come from) and host countries. In recipient economies, migrants help solve shortages of labor and specific skills, while migrants' families back home often receive additional income in the form of remittances, as salaries abroad can be multiples of those in home economies. Returning migrants can bring back new skills and ideas.

International trade, migration, and investment interact in complex ways. Global value chains (GVCs) leverage the efficiencies brought about by cross-border trade and investment, and migration accelerates knowledge spillovers across borders. Recent research suggests that immigration can reduce incentives of recipient countries to automate or move production offshore (Danzer, Feuerbaum, and Gaessler 2020; Olney and Pozzoli 2021).

In sum, trade, foreign investment, and migration spread knowledge and production technologies across borders but, in doing so, may amplify the adverse effects of technological change on inequality. Structural change induced by trade, investment, and migration means reallocation of resources, producing losers as well as winners.

Structural Transformation Produces Winners and Losers

Distributional changes are important in influencing the public perception of globalization. Where gains from trade and foreign investment were not—or were not perceived to be—broadly shared, public backlash often followed. In advanced economies, trade came to be closely associated with offshoring, manufacturing job losses, and stagnant wages. Figure 17 illustrates such popular sentiments through a word cloud based on searches for "globalization" and its synonyms in The Economist since 2001: "inequality," "losers," "poor," and "rich" are somewhat more prominent than positive characterizations such as "benefits," "growth," or "good."

Support for Globalization is Typically Higher in Poorer Economies

Support for trade has, so far, been generally higher in emerging markets and developing economies than in advanced economies.

Figure 17: News Coverage of Globalization

Note: Based on articles from *The Economist*, 2001–2021, containing the word "globalization" or synonyms, excluding common and COVID-19–related terms.

Sources: *The Economist* and authors' calculations.

Trade is more likely to be seen as creating jobs, increasing wages, and decreasing prices by respondents in lower-income economies (Figure 18). The difference is, to a great extent, driven by those on lower incomes, with those on higher incomes and living in urban areas universally more likely to have favorable views of trade and investment. In advanced economies, however, the relationship between income and views on globalization is stronger.

The rest of the chapter looks at trade, investment, and migration in emerging markets, drawing on rich firm- and individual-level data to examine how the forces have influenced inequality as well as growth and speculate about the future of cross-border economic ties. The chapter then reviews policy options for more inclusive trade, investment, and migration.

The analysis supplements Chapter 2, complementing the shorter-term focus on the effects of the COVID-19 crisis and recovery with a longer-term perspective and linking trade, foreign investments, and migration to inequality. The analysis echoes many of the challenges presented in Chapter 2, including emerging markets needing to move beyond attracting foreign investments and participating in GVCs solely based on their labor cost advantages, emphasizing the importance of skills, infrastructure, and regional cooperation.

Figure 18: Views on Trade

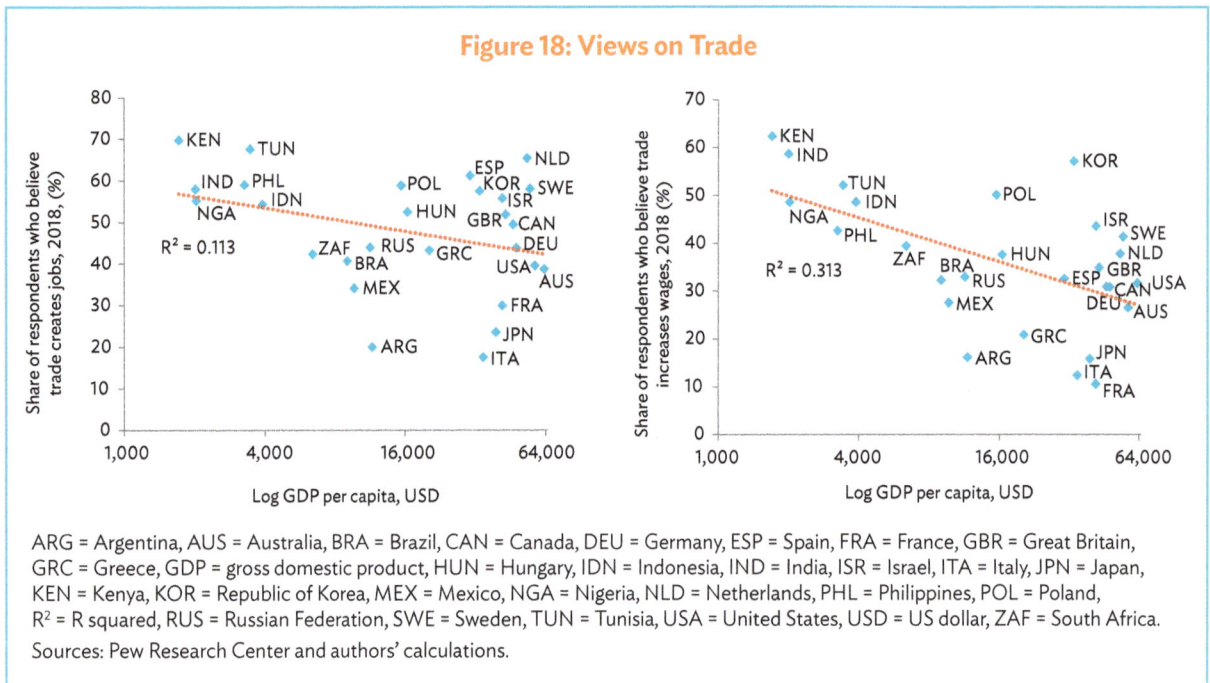

ARG = Argentina, AUS = Australia, BRA = Brazil, CAN = Canada, DEU = Germany, ESP = Spain, FRA = France, GBR = Great Britain, GRC = Greece, GDP = gross domestic product, HUN = Hungary, IDN = Indonesia, IND = India, ISR = Israel, ITA = Italy, JPN = Japan, KEN = Kenya, KOR = Republic of Korea, MEX = Mexico, NGA = Nigeria, NLD = Netherlands, PHL = Philippines, POL = Poland, R² = R squared, RUS = Russian Federation, SWE = Sweden, TUN = Tunisia, USA = United States, USD = US dollar, ZAF = South Africa.
Sources: Pew Research Center and authors' calculations.

Trade and Inequality

Trade improves productivity, brings aggregate benefits.

Openness to trade is expected to increase productivity growth by allowing countries to specialize in areas of their comparative advantage, improving global allocation of resources and providing firms with access to larger markets (Ohlin 1933, Ricardo 1817, Samuelson 1939). In the longer term, trade can enable knowledge spillovers, provide access to improved technologies, strengthen incentives to innovate, and prompt improvements in institutions and policies that underpin international competitiveness. Technological differences between countries can thus confer mutual trading benefits. Each country can benefit, assuming that reallocation of resources is sufficiently swift—a requirement discussed below in greater detail.

Numerous studies have documented the positive impact of trade liberalization on productivity, through reallocation to more productive firms and improvements within firms.[12] Trade has been shown to increase competition and innovation and to lower prices (Bustos 2011; Bloom et al. 2015; Costinot and Rodriguez-Clare 2014; De Loecker 2013; Coe and Helpman 1995; Coe, Helpman, and Hoffmaister 2009; Lileeva and Trefler 2010; and Lumenga-Neso et al. 2005). Some cross-country studies found that trade openness can reduce long-run unemployment and poverty, although the impact depends on institutions and policies (Dollar and Kraay 2004; Dollar et al. 2016; Dutt et al. 2009; Felbermayr et al. 2011; and IMF, World Bank, and WTO 2017).

But gains are uneven.

Notwithstanding aggregate benefits, some industries gain as a result of technological change while others contract. Some workers become worse off even though aggregate benefits would be sufficient to compensate them for their losses. The benefits typically accrue to the country's abundant factors, such as owners of capital (technologies) and highly skilled labor in advanced economies.

In contrast, in emerging markets and developing economies, the impact of trade is less clear-cut. Given the economies' specialization in lower-skilled labor, trade could, in principle, lower inequality. However, newer trade theories focus on the gains from trade within industries, emphasizing economies of scale in production and competition across firms within an industry, where only the most productive find it profitable to export (Krugman 1981, Melitz 2003). The situation results in reallocation across firms as profits and wages in exporters rise while less productive firms contract or exit. Average industry productivity rises as a result, but so may inequality among individuals and across geographic areas.

Most empirical studies found evidence that trade liberalization raised inequality in emerging markets and developing economies, driven by the increase in earnings of better-educated

---

[12]   See surveys by Harrison and Rodriguez-Clare (2010), De Loecker and Goldberg (2014), and Melitz and Redding (2014).

workers relative to those with lower levels of education.[13] Skill premiums increased more in emerging markets, which are relatively more skill-abundant, than in developing economies (Behar 2016, Goldberg and Pavcnik 2007, Meschi and Vivarelli 2008). Wage differentials across firms widened as exporters raised wages faster than non-exporters (Helpman, Itskhoki, Muendler, and Redding 2016; Helpman, Itskhoki, and Redding 2010). Evidence from the Enterprise Surveys across a sample of 67 emerging markets and developing economies suggests that exporting firms employ a higher share of skilled production workers than do non-exporters (taking into account firm size, sector, and other characteristics).

Trade can accelerate the impact of technological change by increasing skill premiums. The Enterprise Surveys showed that the shares of highly skilled workers have increased over time, and in non-exporters as well, albeit more slowly than in exporters. Trade has been correlated with capital inflows, which tend to complement skilled labor (Goldberg and Pavcnik 2007).

Reallocation of labor is often costly and slow.

Aggregate gains from trade crucially depend on smooth reallocation of resources as more productive firms displace less efficient ones. In theory, workers who have lost their jobs in contracting industries could find new ones in expanding sectors.

In practice, numerous studies have documented that reallocation is difficult and costly. Switching occupations may require expensive retraining. Displaced workers are often older, with lower skills and less education, making it harder to find reemployment in alternative industries (Autor et al. 2014; Kletzer 2001; Notowidigdo 2011; OECD 2005, 2012). Industries are often concentrated regionally, but high costs of moving, differences in housing costs, imperfect access to finance, social ties, and sometimes government restrictions may all weigh on geographic mobility, more so in poorer economies (Artuc, Lederman, and Porto 2015; Goldberg and Pavcnik 2007; McCaig 2011; Pavcnik 2017; and Topalova 2007, 2010).

As a result, workers in affected firms, industries, and regions may face prolonged unemployment, poorer health outcomes, and lower educational achievements by children (Altindag and Mocan 2010, Autor et al. 2015, Davis and Von Watcher 2011, Giuliano and Spilimbergo 2009, Oreopoulos et al. 2008, and Pierce and Schott 2016).

The impact of trade is geographically concentrated.

As trade benefits some sectors while hurting others, and industries are often geographically clustered, the effects of trade are often highly local. Regions with a high concentration of export-oriented industries have been found to benefit significantly from trade (Amiti and Davis 2011; Chiquiar 2008; Costa, Garred, and Pessoa 2016; Erten and Leight 2017; McCaig 2011; Oster and Steinberg 2013). In contrast, regions exposed to import competition have

---

[13]   For early studies of the effects of globalization on inequality in developing countries, see Cornia and Kiiski (2002), Galbraith and Kum (2002), Lustig and Kanbur (1999), Milanovic (2005), and Ravallion (2001). Most early work focused on the effects of trade liberalization on income distribution in Latin America. See Arbache (1999); Behrman et al. (2003); Harrison and Hanson (1999); Robertson (2000); Attanasio, Goldberg, and Pavcnik (2004); Barro (2000); Costinot and Vogel (2010); Dix-Carneiro and Kovak (2015); Goldberg and Pavcnik (2005); Lundberg and Squire (1999); Milanovic (2005); Pavcnik (2017); and Ravallion (2001).

been shown to lose out (Baldarrago and Salinas 2017; Dix-Carneiro, Soares, and Ulyssea 2018; Edmonds, Pavcnik, and Topalova 2010; Topalova 2010).[14] Highly localized economic shocks can result in self-reinforcing vicious circles of job losses, firm bankruptcies, lower local government revenues, and more limited provision of local public services, widening regional income disparities (Dix-Carneiro and Kovak 2017).

Figure 19: Changing Specialization Patterns in Trade

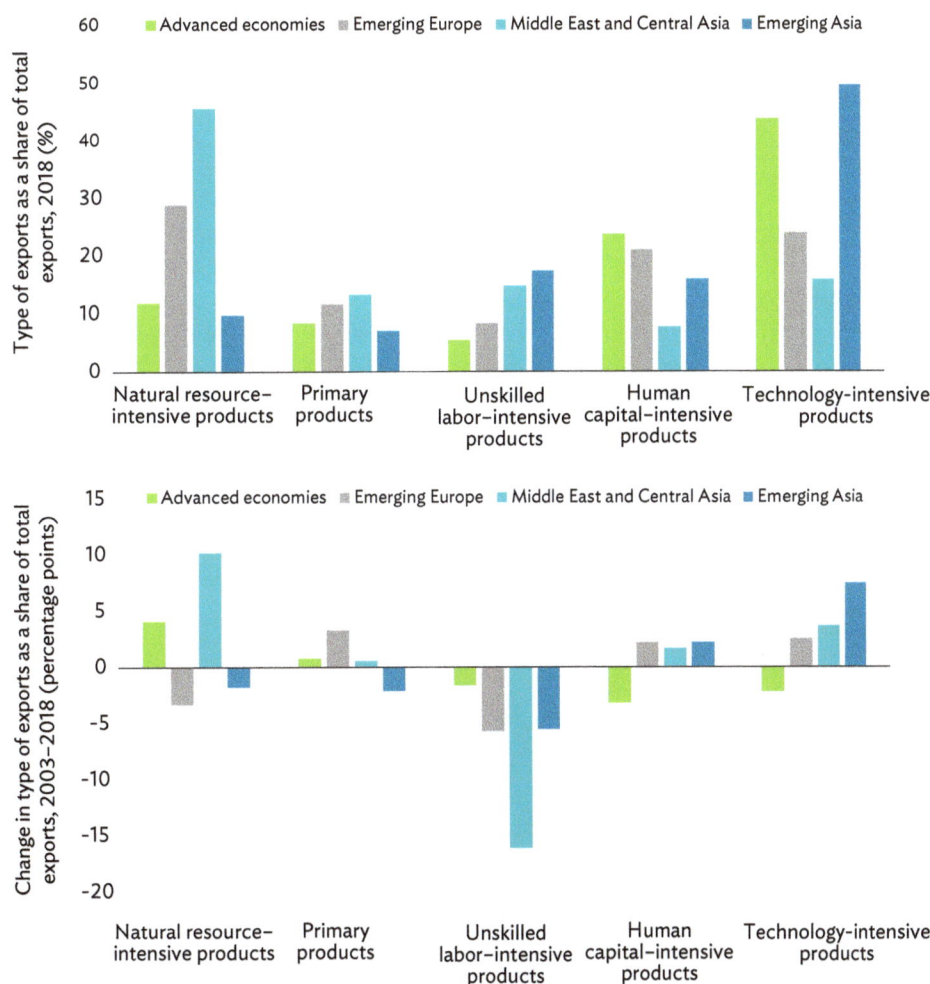

Note: Natural resource–intensive products include energy products, mining commodities and crude-oil products, leather, skin, and wood products; primary products include horticulture products, animal products, and non-mining commodities; unskilled labor–intensive products include textiles and apparel, glassware, pottery, ships, and furniture; human capital–intensive products include manufactured goods; and technology-intensive products include chemical products, machinery and transport equipment, and electrical and optical equipment. Advanced economies include Canada, Cyprus, Estonia, France, Germany, Greece, Italy, Japan, Latvia, Lithuania, the Slovak Republic, Slovenia, the United Kingdom, and the United States. Emerging Europe includes Albania, Belarus, Bosnia and Herzegovina, Bulgaria, Croatia, Hungary, Moldova, Montenegro, North Macedonia, Poland, Romania, the Russian Federation, Serbia, Turkey, and Ukraine. The Middle East and Central Asia include Armenia, Azerbaijan, Egypt, Georgia, Jordan, Kazakhstan, the Kyrgyz Republic, Lebanon, Morocco, Pakistan, Tunisia, and Uzbekistan. Emerging Asia includes the People's Republic of China, India, Indonesia, Malaysia, Mongolia, the Philippines, Thailand, and Viet Nam.

Sources: UN Comtrade (SITC rev.2 3-digit level), Hinloopen and Marrewijk (no date), and authors' calculations.

---

14   See also surveys by Goldberg (2015) and Goldberg and Pavcnik (2007, 2016).

Economies will shift to skill-biased trade.

Trade is likely to become more skill intensive. Figure 19 draws on disaggregated trade data and highlights that skill- and technology-intensive exports account for the bulk of exports of emerging Europe and emerging Asia; the Slovak Republic, for instance, is the world's leading manufacturer of cars in per capita terms. As per capita incomes increase, emerging market exports shift away from their traditional comparative advantage of unskilled labor and move up the value chain, highlighting the importance of the supply of skills keeping up with the structural shift in demand.

Investment and Inequality

Foreign investments boosted growth and productivity.

Declining transport and communication costs have increased the attractiveness of building value chains spanning vast geographies, leading to a spectacular increase in global foreign direct investment (FDI) flows over recent decades. Emerging markets and developing economies have become major players in global production chains (Harding and Javorcik 2012).

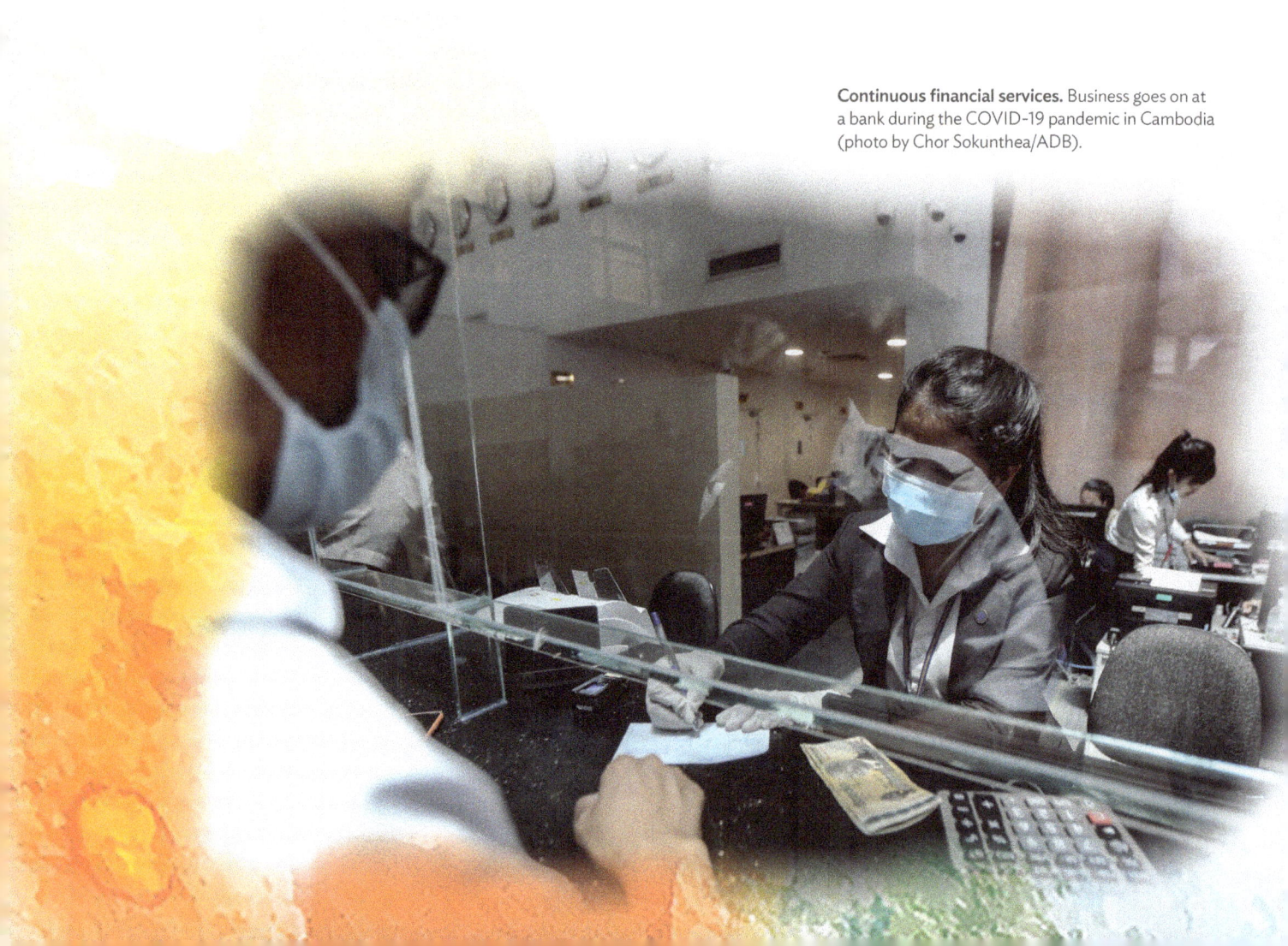

Continuous financial services. Business goes on at a bank during the COVID-19 pandemic in Cambodia (photo by Chor Sokunthea/ADB).

For the recipient economies, FDI can bring much-needed capital and new technologies. Numerous empirical studies have documented the positive impact of FDI inflows on the productivity of domestic firms through contacts between foreign affiliates and their local suppliers in upstream sectors and buyers in downstream sectors, enabling the production of more complex products and export upgrading (Bajgar and Javorcik forthcoming; Harding and Javorcik 2012; Javorcik 2004; and Javorcik, Lo Turco, and Maggioni 2017).

Foreign ownership has been shown to influence firm culture, for instance, through flexible working arrangements, telecommuting, and childcare subsidies (Kodama, Javorcik, and Abe 2018). Foreign firms were, for instance, more likely to introduce remote working arrangements during the COVID-19 crisis. FDI has typically been found to increase aggregate formal employment and wages owing to increased labor productivity (Dinga and Münich 2010; Hale and Xu 2016; Karlsson et al. 2009; Peluffo 2015; Waldkirch, Nunnenkamp, and Bremont 2009; World Bank 2020). Foreign firms are often seen as a source of more stable employment and provide more training to their employees than local firms (Javorcik 2015).

Foreign direct investment contributed to rising inequality.

Like trade, FDI can amplify the effects of technological change on income distribution. Advanced economies typically outsource production in search of lower labor costs. While these activities are relatively low skilled in higher-income economies, the required skill levels may be above average in the receiving, lower-income country. Beyond the direct effects, FDI can create jobs along the supply chain, displace jobs in competitors, enable technology and knowledge spillovers to other firms, and indirectly impact the economy in other ways. On balance, FDI increased the wage gap between skilled and unskilled workers (Feenstra and Hanson 1997, Figini and Görg 2011, Head and Ries 2002, Lee and Wie 2015).

Insights from a rich individual-level survey covering 34 emerging markets and developing economies across emerging Europe and Central Asia suggest that younger, more highly educated workers are more likely to be employed by a foreign firm (Figure 20). For instance, more than 24% of workers in foreign firms have a university degree, compared with 16% of those in domestic private firms. The effects of age and university education remain significant in a regression framework when considering various individual characteristics and respondents' country of residence. Those working for foreign firms are more likely to be in the upper half of the income distribution relative to those working for domestic private firms. They are more likely to have permanent contracts.

Figure 20: Employment in Foreign Firms

Share of workers in a given income decile as a share of all workers in domestic private (foreign) firms (%)

Categories along x-axis: Poorest, 2, 3, 4, 5, 6, 7, 8, 9, Richest

Legend: ■ Domestic private ■ Foreign

Note: Employment based on primary respondents' main job. Deciles are based on those receiving monthly salaries, excluding salaries and benefits. The survey is based on a sample of 34 emerging markets and developing economies.
Sources: Life in Transition Survey 2016 and authors' calculations.

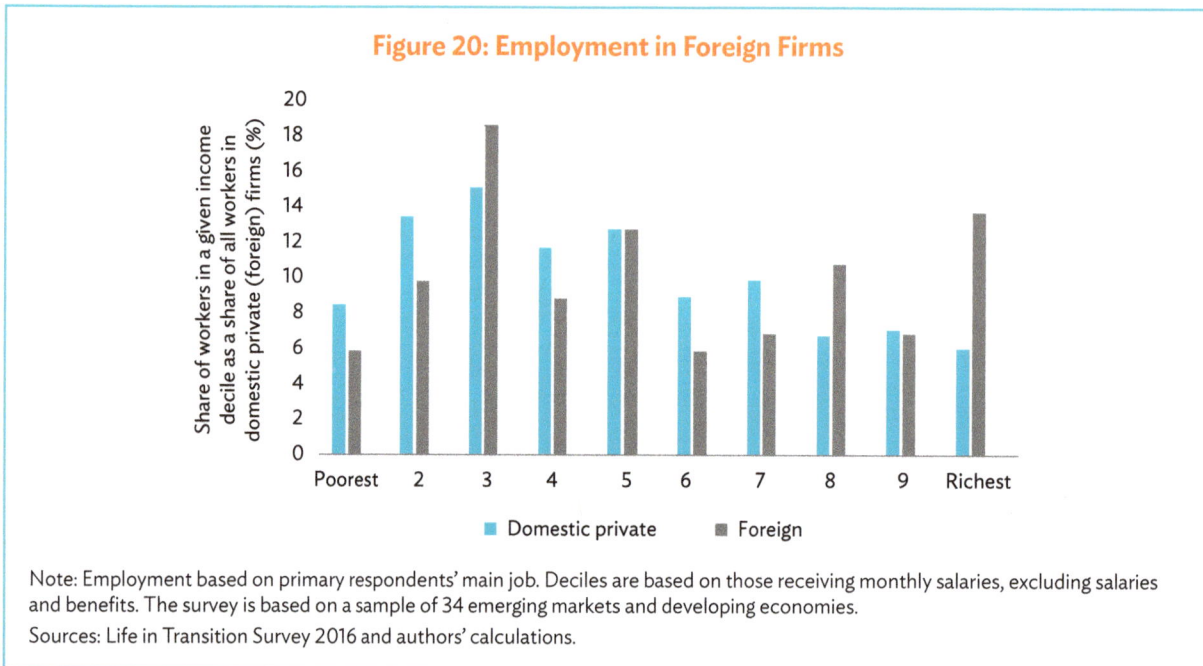

Without foreign direct investment (FDI), the average Gini coefficient (a measure of inequality) in emerging Europe would be some 2 points lower (averaging 30 instead of 32) while average incomes would be 1.2% lower (Figure 21). The calculations are based on the Life in Transition survey and a thought experiment, where those working for foreign firms instead worked for domestic private firms, which pay lower wages. The calculations do not account for any indirect effects of foreign ownership on productivity of other firms. The estimated effect of FDI on inequality is smaller when assuming that the more highly skilled worked for the public sector or emigrated instead, although the estimate does not account for other economy-wide costs of potential distortions or brain drain.

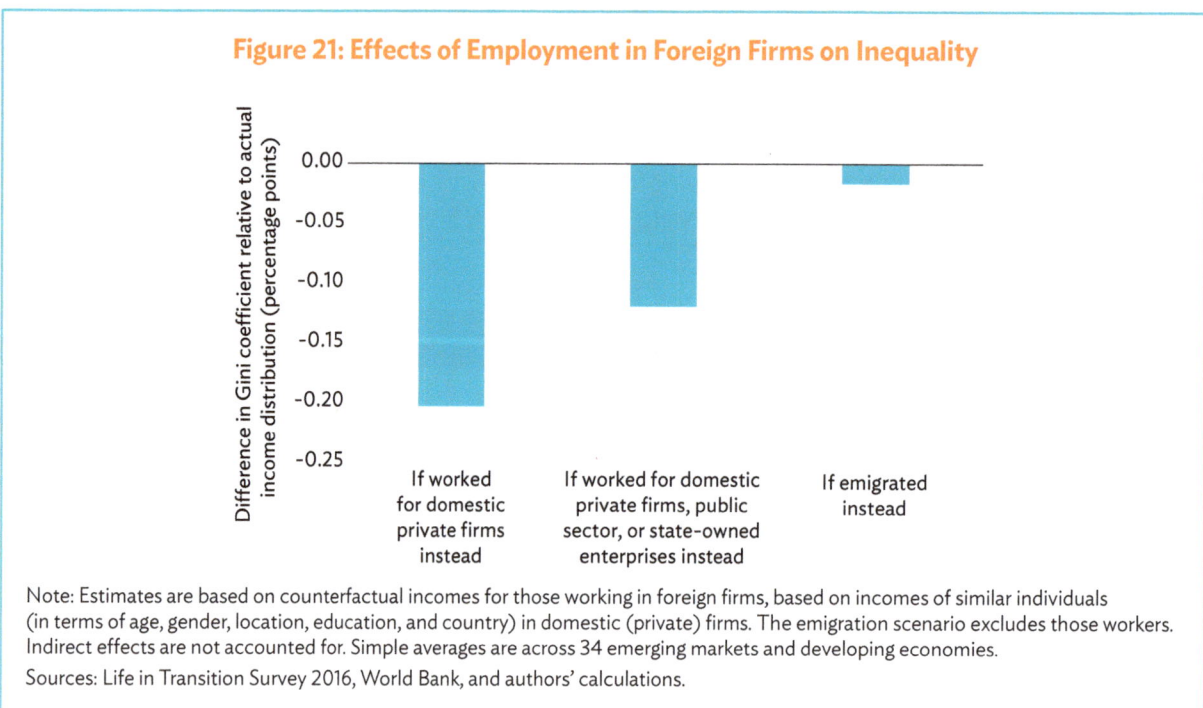

Figure 21: Effects of Employment in Foreign Firms on Inequality

Difference in Gini coefficient relative to actual income distribution (percentage points)

Categories: If worked for domestic private firms instead; If worked for domestic private firms, public sector, or state-owned enterprises instead; If emigrated instead

Note: Estimates are based on counterfactual incomes for those working in foreign firms, based on incomes of similar individuals (in terms of age, gender, location, education, and country) in domestic (private) firms. The emigration scenario excludes those workers. Indirect effects are not accounted for. Simple averages are across 34 emerging markets and developing economies.
Sources: Life in Transition Survey 2016, World Bank, and authors' calculations.

In some instances, FDI in textiles, food processing, and other labor-intensive low-skilled sectors has been found to be associated with lower inequality (Cornia 2016, Cruz et al. 2018, Leamer 1998, Luo 2017).[15] Inequality tended to increase less in countries with higher average levels of education (e.g., Mihaylova 2015), while higher-quality institutions were shown to help maximize the benefits of FDI inflows (Baiashvili and Gattini 2020).

Foreign direct investment has become less labor-intensive.

As with trade, patterns of FDI have been changing, with increased focus on skill-intensive sectors. To track such changes, the following analysis draws on a rich project-level database of FDI inflows into 37 economies in emerging Europe, Central Asia, and southern and eastern Mediterranean.

Greenfield FDI has been a major source of job creation in the region (Figure 22). However, in higher-income economies, such job creation has been slowing as labor costs have risen.[16] New large-scale manufacturing investments have become less common, with the service sector now accounting for most investments.

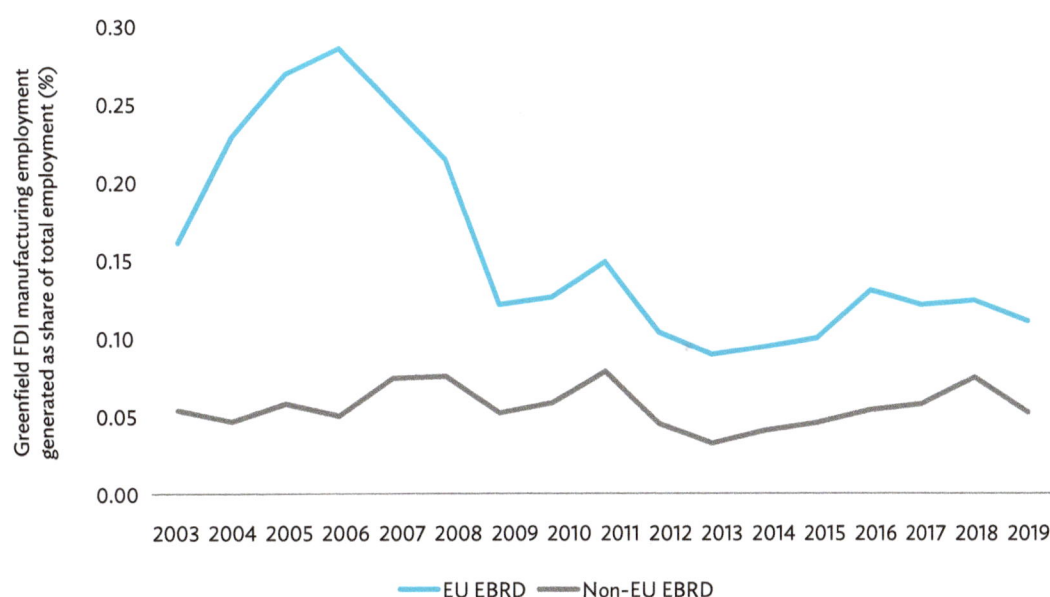

Figure 22: Foreign Direct Investment–Related Job Creation in Manufacturing

EBRD = European Bank for Reconstruction and Development, EU = European Union, FDI = foreign direct investment.
Note: Based on a sample of 37 emerging markets and developing economies.
Sources: CEIC, fDi Markets Database, national authorities, and authors' calculations.

---

[15]   See also Eichengreen et al. (2021) for a review.
[16]   See, for example, Qiang and Kusek (2020) or Haque and Thaku (2013) on implications for the PRC and India.

Despite the shift to services, FDI has become less labor-intensive, creating fewer jobs per million dollars invested (Figure 23) as labor intensity in many sectors has been falling.

Figure 23: Changing Labor Intensity of Greenfield Foreign Direct Investment Inflows

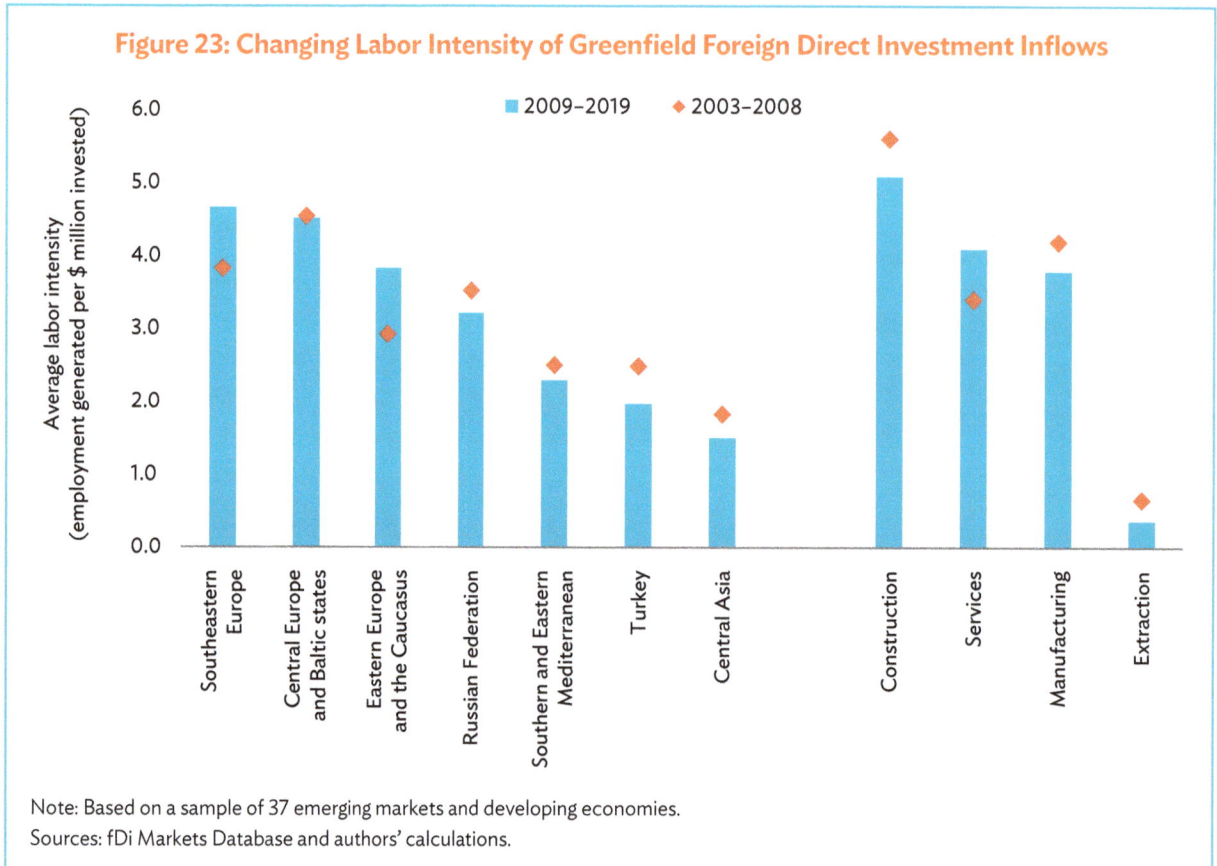

Note: Based on a sample of 37 emerging markets and developing economies.
Sources: fDi Markets Database and authors' calculations.

Some of the drop in labor intensity can be explained by changes in the main source countries of FDI. Inflows from the PRC, predominantly into Central Asia, southern and eastern Mediterranean, the Russian Federation, and the Western Balkans, have increased sharply on the back of the Belt and Road Initiative, although from low initial levels (Figure 24).

While the PRC's projects tend to be larger on average than those of Germany or the US, they are typically less labor-intensive, creating about four instead of five jobs per million US dollars invested (Figure 25). The trend is in line with the PRC's FDI flows often being concentrated in capital-intensive extractive sectors, with a large pool of labor available in the home economy.

Figure 24: Changes in Source Countries of Greenfield Foreign Direct Investment Inflows

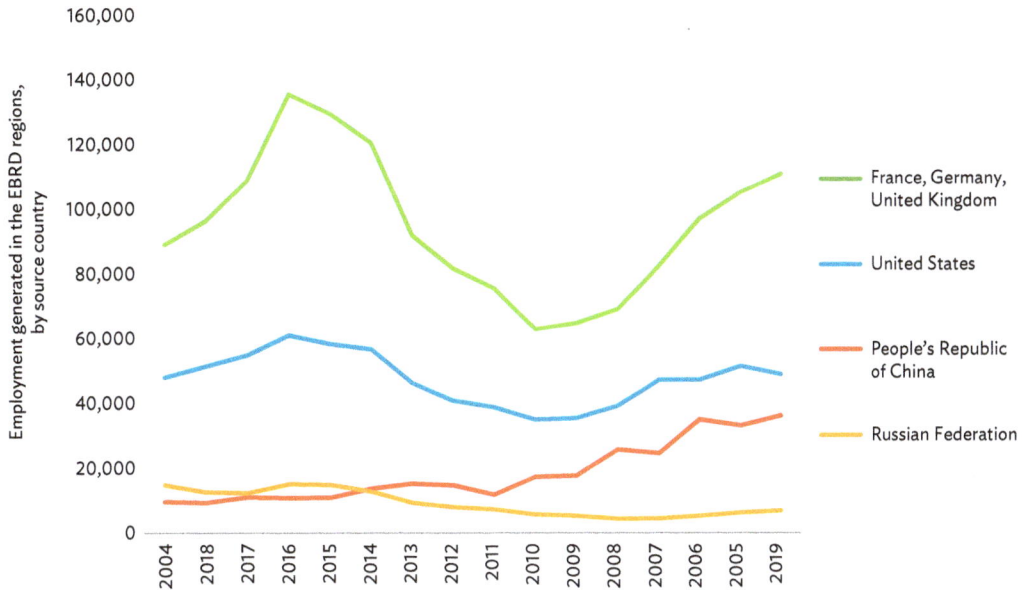

EBRD = European Bank for Reconstruction and Development.
Note: Based on a sample of 37 emerging markets and developing economies.
Sources: fDi Markets Database and authors' calculations.

Figure 25: Size and Labor Intensity of Greenfield Foreign Direct Investment Inflows, by Source Country

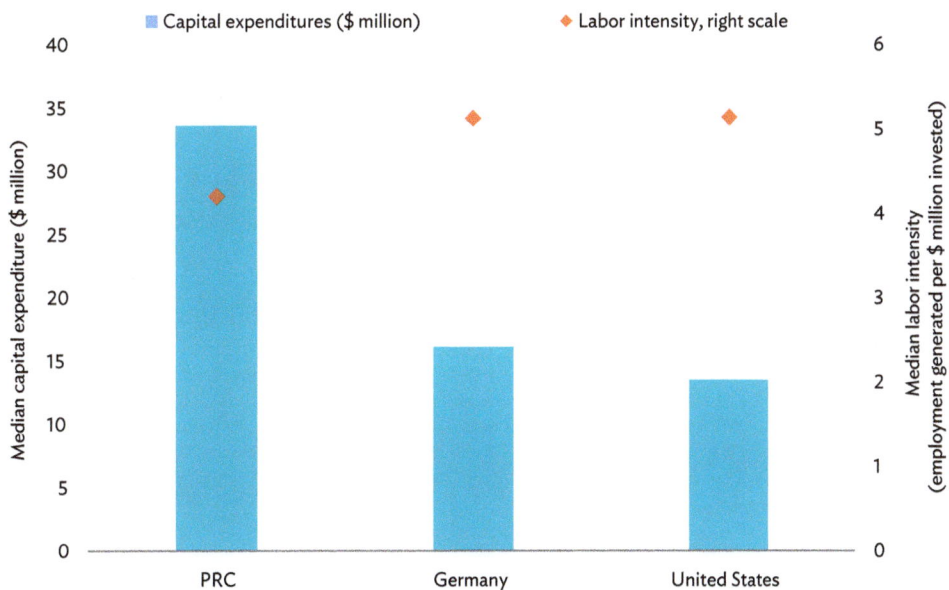

PRC = People's Republic of China.
Note: Based on a sample of 37 emerging markets and developing economies.
Sources: fDi Markets Database and authors' calculations.

Foreign investment has become more skill intensive and spatially concentrated.

Greenfield FDI projects have become more skill intensive (Figure 26), mirroring changes in trade as emerging markets move up value chains.

The effects of FDI are also often highly localized, at least in the short term.[17] Increased demand for highly skilled labor can push up the wages of skilled workers in regions and industries with a higher FDI presence, particularly in emerging and developing countries characterized by limited mobility between regions (Dix-Carneiro and Kovak 2015, Hale and Xu 2016, Pavcnik 2017).

Figure 26: Skill Intensity of Greenfield Foreign Direct Investment Projects

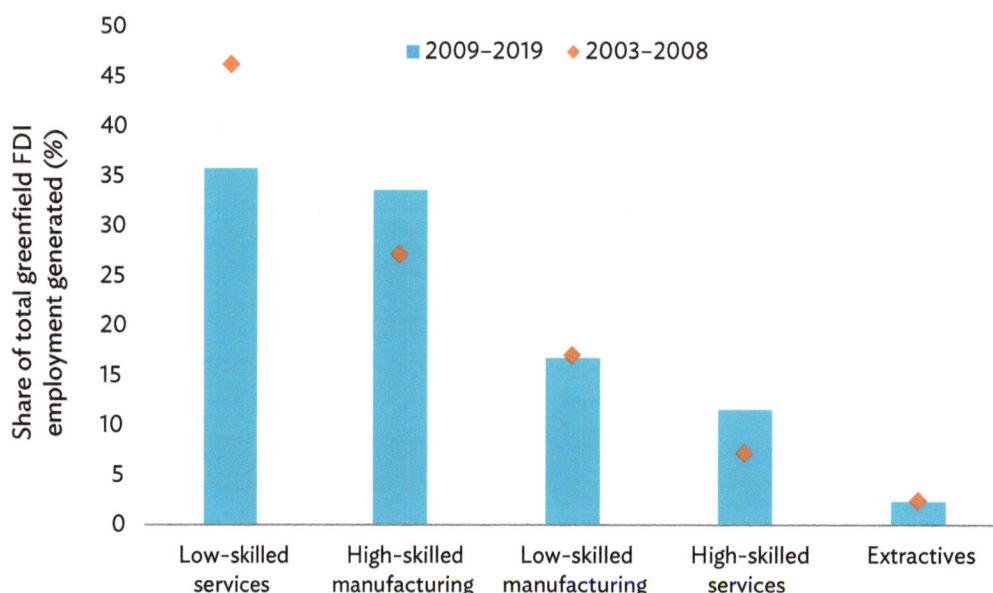

FDI = foreign direct investment.

Notes: Based on a sample of 37 emerging markets and developing economies. The broad sector classification according to skill level is based on Hallward-Driemeier and Nayyar (2017), following the International Standard Industrial Classification (ISIC) rev. 4. Extractives and agriculture include agriculture, forestry and fishing, and mining and quarrying (ISIC 01–09). Low-skilled manufacturing includes food, beverages and tobacco, textiles, clothing and leather, manufacturing of wood, wood and cork products, paper products and printing, furniture, rubber and plastic products, basic metal and metal products and other nonmetallic mineral products, and other manufacturing (ISIC 10–18, 22–25, 31–32). High-skilled manufacturing includes coke and refined petroleum products, chemicals, chemical products, pharmaceuticals, computer electronics, optical products and electronic equipment, machinery and equipment, motor vehicles and other transport equipment (ISIC 19–21, 26–30). Low-skilled services include construction, trade, transportation and storage, accommodation and food service, real estate activities, and administrative and business support services (ISIC 41–53, 55–56, 68, 77–83). High-skilled services include electricity, gas, steam, and air conditioning supply; water supply; sewerage and waste management; information and communication; finance and insurance activities; professional, scientific, and technical services; education, human health and social work; and arts, entertainment, and recreation (ISIC 35–39, 58–66, 69–75, 85–88, and 90–93).

Sources: fDi Markets Database and authors' calculations.

---

[17]   Agglomeration effects driving FDI flows are the subject of much literature. See, for example, Cantwell and Piscitello (2005); Crozet, Mayer, and Mucchielli (2004); Driffield and Munday (2000); Guimaraes, Figueiredo, and Woodward (2000); Head, Ries, and Swenson (1999); and Woodward (1992).

FDI inflows have thus been associated with increases in geographical inequality (McLaren and Yoo 2016; Nunnenkamp, Schweickert, and Wiebelt 2007). Evidence from the project database suggests that early greenfield FDI investments in emerging Europe, Central Asia, and southern and eastern Mediterranean were dominated by construction projects in capital cities, followed by more dispersed manufacturing projects in the boom years of the early 2000s. However, the increasing importance of services increased the concentration of inflows in major cities. Richer regions (including capital cities) have seen greater increases in greenfield FDI jobs, considering differences in regions' populations.

Greenfield FDI projects have become more clustered. Moran's I, a measure of spatial autocorrelation, ranges from –1 for perfectly dispersed projects through 0 for randomly distributed projects to 1 for perfectly clustered projects. Clustering based on the measure appears to have increased over time, including within individual sectors, with construction projects being most concentrated (Figure 27). Clustering increased within most countries, except in commodity-rich economies such as Kazakhstan and the Russian Federation.

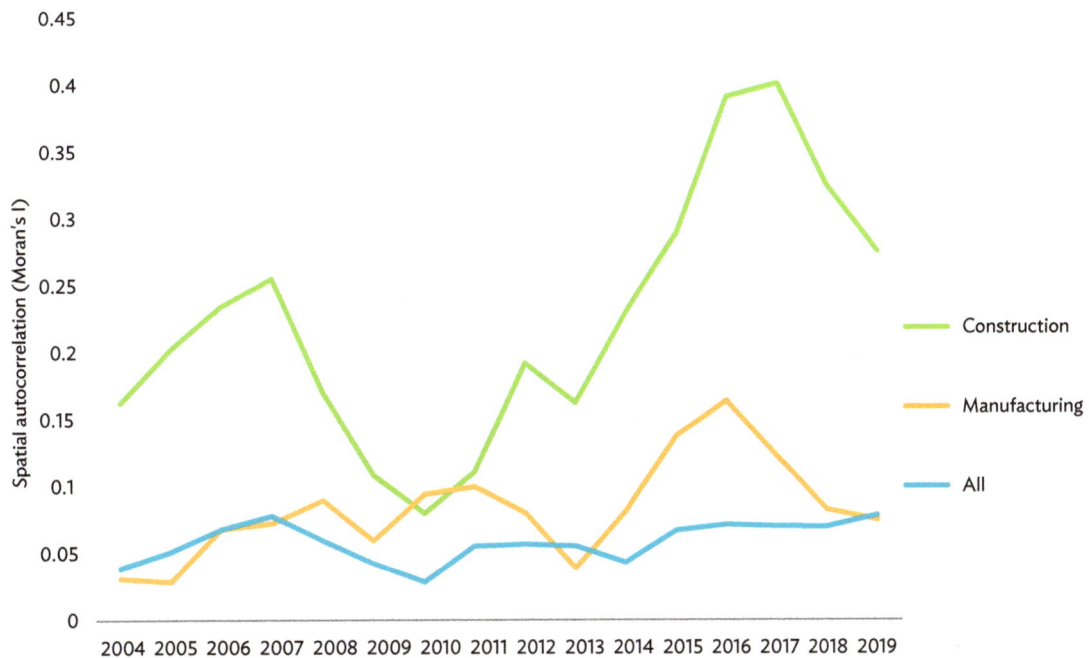

Figure 27: Spatial Clustering of Greenfield Foreign Direct Investment Inflows

Notes: Based on a subset of projects with information on destination city name (about 63% of the sample). Moran's I is calculated using an exponential spatial weight matrix. Lines denote 3-year centered moving averages.
Sources: fDi Markets Database and authors' calculations.

Migration and Inequality

Migration can benefit home countries.

Outmigration reduces labor supply in home countries, an effect often exacerbated by brain drain—selective outmigration of those with higher levels of education (Grogger and Hanson 2011, IMF 2016). However, networks developed by migrants can support the integration of migrants' countries of origin into GVCs (Burchardi, Chaney, and Hassan 2016; OECD 2017; Parsons and Vezina 2016).[18] Remittances constitute an important source of external financing for many developing economies. The prospects of migration can incentivize individuals to invest in human capital.

Migration and remittances could become more pro-poor.

Little is known, however, about the effects of migration and remittances on inequality in emerging markets and developing economies. The effects depend on who migrates and which households receive remittances. While some studies found that migration and remittances increase inequality (Adams 2006, Adams et al. 2008, Barham and Boucher 1998, Bouoiyour and Miftah 2014, Koczan and Loyola 2021, Möllers and Meyer 2014), others found the opposite (Acosta et al. 2006, Brown and Jimenez 2007, Gubert et al. 2010, Margolis et al. 2013, Mughal and Anwar 2012, Taylor et al. 2009) or no significant effect (Beyene 2014, Yang and Martinez 2005).

These conflicting findings could be driven by changing effects over time. "Pioneer" migrants (who face higher costs of migration) may be richer than later migrants, who benefit from falling costs of migration because of improved access to labor markets as migrant networks expand (Stark, Taylor, and Yitzhaki 1986).[19] Migration and resulting remittances thus first increase then decrease inequality in sending countries. In a cross-section, outmigration was associated with higher inequality in sending countries with a more recent migration history (Stark, Taylor, and Yitzhaki 1988).

Figure 28 draws on the household survey covering 34 economies across emerging Europe and Central Asia. Participants were asked if they intended to emigrate in the next 12 months and about their household income. The characteristics of those who stated their intentions to migrate closely match the characteristics of actual migrants.

The analysis reveals that in countries with a short migration history, the rich are significantly more likely to express a desire to migrate than the poor. In contrast, in countries with a longer migration history, migration intentions are more evenly distributed across the population. As more people have already migrated, many personally know someone who has moved abroad. Information and networks lower the costs of migration, making the option more accessible to poorer households. Intentions to migrate are generally higher in urban than in rural areas

---

[18]   See also Koczan et al. (2021) for a review.

[19]   See also Clemens (2014), De Haas et al. (2018), and Ortega and Peri (2013) on how migration from low- and middle-income countries increases with country development.

Figure 28: Intention to Migrate by Income Decile and Location

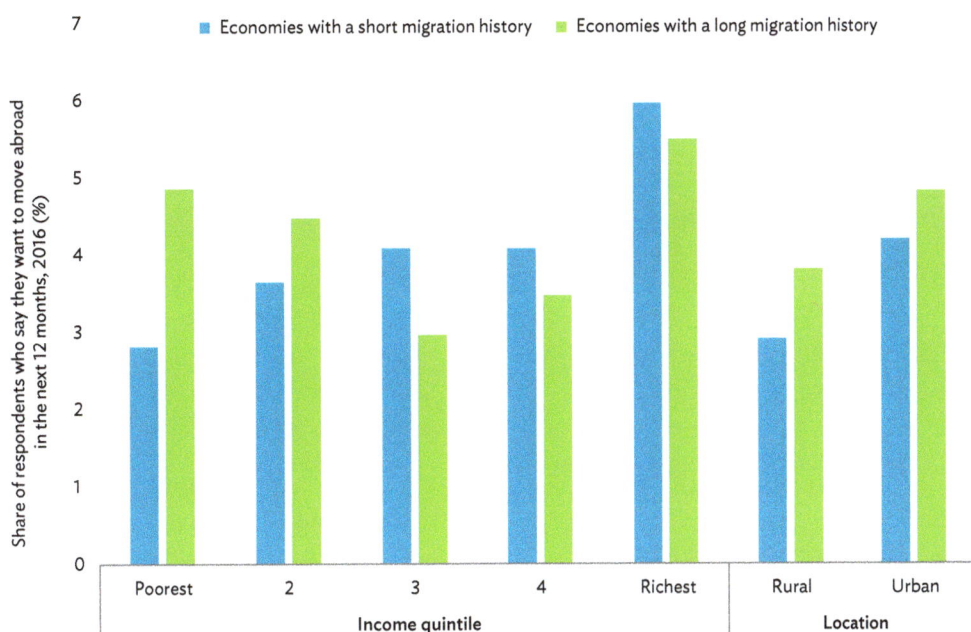

Note: Long (short) migration history refers to countries with migrant stocks abroad exceeding 10% of their domestic population in 1990 (2010). Based on a sample of 34 emerging markets and developing economies.

Sources: Life in Transition Survey 2016, United Nations, and authors' calculations.

(consistent with typically higher urban incomes), but the difference is less pronounced in countries with a longer migration history.

In contrast with trade and FDI patterns, migration flows could become more pro-poor if migration decisions, and thus remittances, became more uniformly distributed across higher- and lower-income households in sending countries.

Remittances have a stabilizing effect.

Migration and remittance flows have historically been among the most stable international flows. They tend to persist even in times of crises and when they are difficult or costly to send. While differences in living standards across countries are an important factor driving migration (often east to west and south to north), year-to-year fluctuations in economic activity tend to matter little, in contrast to the highly pro-cyclical private international capital flows. Remittances compensated for the loss of assets after disasters triggered by natural hazards (Arouri et al. 2015, Davies 2008, Fagen 2006, Halliday 2006, Mohapatra et al. 2009, Suleri and Savage 2006, World Bank 2006, Wu 2006) and functioned as insurance during other price and income shocks (Ambrosius and Cuecuecha 2013, Combes and Ebeke 2011, Combes et al. 2014, and De Brauw et al. 2013).

The COVID-19 pandemic, however, resulted not only in widespread job losses (including among migrants, limiting their ability to send money home) but also widespread restrictions on travel. In the short term, the pandemic caused sharp drops in migration and remittances and significant return migration in some countries. Remittances to many economies, however, appear to be recovering already.

Policies to Promote Inclusive Trade, Investment, and Migration

Cross-border economic integration delivers productivity growth. The overall gains from trade and FDIs can thus be leveraged further by policies that reduce barriers to the international flow of goods and factors of production, including through investments in infrastructure and logistics or streamlined customs and investment procedures (Box 8). Multilateral development banks (MDBs) can support and coordinate such multilateral efforts.

However, concerted policy effort is needed to ensure that such growth is inclusive and that gains from cross-border trade, investment, and migration can be broadly shared.

Box 8: Logistics and Connectivity: Central Asia's Challenges

Central Asia is at the heart of Eurasian connectivity. The potential is enormous to strengthen the subregion as a key transport corridor, which will, in turn, support growth in corridor economies. However, shortcomings in physical infrastructure, regulation, and quality of logistics management hold back the growth of international trade.

Inefficiencies in logistics—reflecting underdeveloped warehouse services and lack of highly trained professionals—can inflate trade costs far above the direct costs associated with tariffs and taxes, as do complicated and time-consuming customs procedures. Infrastructure investment needs are estimated to be in excess of 80% of gross domestic product in Mongolia; about 30% in Tajikistan, the Kyrgyz Republic, and Turkmenistan; and 20% in Kazakhstan. Existing assets deteriorate fast, given limited allocation of public funds for infrastructure maintenance and construction. As a result, the quality of infrastructure and logistics services in Central Asia is perceived as low, according to World Bank data.

With limited fiscal space in many economies, identifying projects with the highest economic rates of return is of the utmost importance, as is preparing projects in line with international standards, to ensure transparent and efficient use of funds and increase the likelihood of attracting international investors. These efforts need to be accompanied by developing skills in project preparation and assessment.

Source: Idil Bilgic-Alpaslan, European Bank for Reconstruction and Development.

Enable reallocation of resources in the economy.

Reallocation of labor and capital across firms, sectors, and geographic areas can be supported by strengthening social safety nets and education, including programs of vocational training and mid-career retraining in cooperation with private sector employers; improving information on jobs and skill certification; phasing out restrictions on in-country labor mobility; and removing barriers to financial inclusion (Abebe et al. 2017, Beam 2016, Jensen 2012, World Bank 2020). MDBs can support economies by providing policy advice and easing the exchange of experiences and know-how across countries.

Ensure that gains are broadly shared.

Targeted policies supporting redistribution of income can help tackle rising inequality (including geographical inequality). Public investments in infrastructure and logistics can help create the preconditions for private sector investment, including FDI, in disadvantaged regions. MDBs can support such efforts by financing investments in infrastructure, allowing firms and workers in remote areas to access foreign markets and enabling their participation in GVCs. Such efforts can help make regions more attractive to FDI, reducing their concentration in capital cities and already better-off regions.

Strengthening the absorptive capacity of domestic economies can increase the potential benefits of trade and FDI. Examples of measures include programs that foster linkages between foreign-sponsored production facilities and local suppliers, development of business networks and institutional partnerships that help diffuse information, and on-the-job training programs and investment in hard infrastructure and soft skills needed for domestic firms to benefit from knowledge spillovers. Policy interventions are likely to be more successful where they focus on boosting the absorptive capacity of the economy rather than individual firms (Amann and Virmani 2014; Harding and Javorcik 2011, 2012; Javorcik, Lo Turco, and Maggioni 2017; Perea and Stephenson 2018; Te Velde and Xenogiani 2007; World Bank 2020). MDBs can leverage investments in education and advise countries on targeting sectors best suited to their skill mix.

Investment promotion agencies can ensure strong alignment of trade and FDI with the country's skill base. They should start by assessing the country's skill base, possibly through a job diagnostic survey. Sectors and technologies can be targeted based on skill endowments and priorities for skill development in line with a national development strategy (World Bank 2020, Perea and Stephenson 2018). MDBs can advise on policy and promote regional cooperation and the exchange of information and experience.

Spillovers from FDI in services to domestic firms can be increased by focusing on export-oriented sectors or ones with strong links to manufacturing. For instance, FDI in professional business services, finance, logistics, or utilities (such as power, telecommunications, or transportation) is likely to have a bigger effect on domestic manufacturing firms' productivity than investment in other service sectors (Arnold et al. 2016; Arnold, Javorcik, and Mattoo 2011; Duggan, Rahardja, and Varela 2013; World Bank 2020). Finally, regions within economies can benefit from a coordinated approach to investment promotion and tax incentives (Harding and Javorcik 2012).

Conclusions

While many emerging markets once relied on their comparative advantages in unskilled labor, exports and FDI are likely to become more capital and skill intensive as countries' incomes grow, resulting in a shift to more sophisticated products. The development is welcome: trade, FDI, and migration boost productivity by spreading knowledge and new production technologies across borders.

However, the structural transformation facilitated by trade and FDI is likely to affect income distribution and increase inequality, as benefits may mostly accrue to the more highly skilled and those living in richer, urban locations.

Gains from globalization can be used to fund policies that spread the benefits of international economic integration, which, in turn, can strengthen popular support for the cross-border flow of goods, capital, and labor. Such policies need to be cognizant of the disproportionate effects of trade, FDI, and migration on workers with certain skills and those in specific sectors or geographical areas.

References

Abebe, G., S. Caria, M. Fafchamps, P. Falco, S. Franklin, S. Quinn, and F. Shilpi. 2017. Job Fairs: Matching Firms and Workers in a Field Experiment in Ethiopia. *Policy Research Working Paper*. 8092. Washington, DC: World Bank.

Acosta, P., C. Calderon, P. Fajnzylber, and H. Lopez. 2008. What Is the Impact of International Remittances on Poverty and Inequality in Latin America? *World Development*. 36 (1). pp. 89–114.

Adams, R. H. Jr. 2006. Remittances and Poverty in Ghana. *Policy Research Working Paper*. 3838. Washington, DC: World Bank.

Adams, R., A. Cuecuecha, and J. Page. 2008. The Impact of Remittances on Poverty and Inequality in Ghana. *Policy Research Working Paper*. 4732. Washington, DC: World Bank.

Altindag, D. T. and N. H. Mocan. 2010. Joblessness and Perceptions about the Effectiveness of Democracy. *NBER Working Paper*. 15994. Cambridge, MA: National Bureau of Economic Research.

Amann, E. and S. Virmani. 2014. Foreign Direct Investment and Reverse Technology Spillovers: The Effect on Total Factor Productivity. *OECD Journal: Economic Studies*. 2014 (1). pp. 129–53.

Ambrosius, C. and A. Cuecuecha. 2013. Are Remittances a Substitute for Credit? Carrying the Financial Burden of Health Shocks in National and Transnational Households. *World Development*. 46. pp. 143–52.

Amiti, M. and D. Davis. 2012. Trade, Firms, and Wages: Theory and Evidence. *Review of Economic Studies*. 79 (1). pp. 1–36.

Arbache, J. S. 1999. How Do Economic Reforms Affect the Dispersion and Structure: The Case of an Industrialising Country Labor Market. Paper presented at the 1999 Royal Society conference, 29 March –1 April.

Arnold, J. M., B. Javorcik, M. Lipscomb, and A. Mattoo. 2016. Services Reform and Manufacturing Performance: Evidence from India. *The Economic Journal*. 126 (590). pp. 1–39.

Arnold, J. M., B. Javorcik, and A. Mattoo. 2011. Does Services Liberalization Benefit Manufacturing Firms? Evidence from the Czech Republic. *Policy Research Working Paper*. Washington, DC: World Bank.

Arouri, M., C. Nguyen, and A. B. Youssef. 2015. Natural Disasters, Household Welfare, and Resilience: Evidence from Rural Vietnam. *World Development*. 70. pp. 59–77.

Artuc, E., D. Lederman, and G. Porto. 2015. A Mapping of Labor Mobility Costs in the Developing World. *Journal of International Economics*. 95, (1). pp. 28–41.

Attanasio, O., P. Goldberg, and N. Pavcnik. 2004. Trade Reforms and Wage Inequality in Colombia. *Journal of Development Economics*. 74 (4). pp. 331–66.

Autor, D., D. Dorn, and G. Hansen. 2016. The China Shock: Learning from Labor Market Adjustment to Large Changes in Trade. *Annual Review of Economics*. 8.

Autor, D., D. Dorn, G. Hanson, and J. Song. 2014. Trade Adjustment: Worker Level Evidence. *Quarterly Journal of Economics*. 129.

Bacchetta, M., V. Cerra, R. Piermartini, and M. Smeets. 2021. Trade and Inclusive Growth. *IMF Working Paper*. 2021/074. Washington, DC: International Monetary Fund.

Baiashvili, T. and L. Gattini. 2020. Impact of FDI on Economic Growth: The Role of Country Income Levels and Institutional Strength. *European Investment Bank Working Paper*. 2020/02. Luxembourg: European Investment Bank.

Bajgar, M. and B. Javorcik. 2020. Climbing the Rungs of the Quality Ladder: FDI and Domestic Exporters in Romania. *The Economic Journal*. 130 (628). pp. 937–55.

Baldarrago, E. and G. Salinas. 2017. Trade Liberalization in Peru: Adjustment Costs Amidst High Labor Mobility. *IMF Working Paper*. 17/47. Washington, DC: International Monetary Fund.

Barham, B. and S. Boucher. 1998. Migration, Remittances, and Inequality: Estimating the Net Effects of Migration on Income Distribution. *Journal of Development Economics*. 55. pp. 307–31.

Barro, R. 2000. Inequality and Growth in a Panel of Countries. *Journal of Economic Growth*. 5 (1). pp. 5–32

Beam, E. A. 2016. Do Job Fairs Matter? Experimental Evidence on the Impact of Job-Fair Attendance. *Journal of Development Economics*. 120. pp. 32–40.

Behar, A. 2016. The Endogenous Skill Bias of Technical Change and Wage Inequality in Developing Countries. *The Journal of International Trade & Economic Development*. 25 (8). pp. 1101–21.

Behrman, J., N. Birdsall, and M. Szekely. 2003. Economic Policy and Wage Differentials Latin America. *Center for Global Development Working Paper*. 29. Washington, DC.

Beyene, B. M. 2014. The Effects of International Remittances on Poverty and Inequality in Ethiopia. *The Journal of Development Studies*. 50 (10). pp. 1380–96.

Bloom, N., M. Draca, and J. van Reenen. 2015. Trade Induced Technical Change: The Impact of Chinese Imports on Innovation, Diffusion, and Productivity. *Review of Economic Studies*. 83.

Bouoiyour, J. and A. Miftah. 2014. The Effects of Remittances on Poverty and Inequality: Evidence from Rural Southern Morocco. *MPRA Paper*. 55686. Munich Personal RePEc Archive.

Brown, R. P. C. and E. Jimenez. 2007. Estimating the Net Effects of Migration and Remittances on Poverty and Inequality: Comparison of Fiji and Tonga. *UNU-WIDER Research Paper*. 2007/23. Helsinki: United Nations University World Institute for Development Economics Research.

Burchardi, K. B., T. Chaney, and T. A. Hassan. 2016. Migrants, Ancestors, and Investments. *NBER Working Paper*. 21847. Cambridge, MA: National Bureau of Economic Research.

Bustos, P. 2011. Trade Liberalization, Exports, and Technology Upgrading: Evidence on the Impact of MERCOSUR on Argentinian Firms. *American Economic Review*. 101, pp. 304–40.

Cantwell, J. and L. Piscitello. 2005. Recent Location of Foreign-Owned Research and Development Activities by Large Multinational Corporations in the European Regions: The Role of Spillovers and Externalities. *Regional Studies*. 39 (1). pp. 1–16.

Chiquiar, D. 2008. Globalization, Regional Wage Differentials and the Stolper-Samuelson Theorem: Evidence from Mexico. *Journal of International Economics*. 74. pp. 70–93.

Clemens, M. A. 2014. Does Development Reduce Migration? In *International Handbook on Migration and Economic Development*. Cheltenham, UK and Northampton, MA, United States: Edward Elgar Publishing.

Coe, D. and E. Helpman. 1995. International R&D Spillovers. *European Economic Review*. 39 (5). pp. 859–87.

Coe, D., E. Helpman, and A. Hoffmaister. 2009. International R&D Spillovers and Institutions. *European Economic Review*. 53 (7). pp. 723–41.

Combes, J.-L. and C. Ebeke. 2011. Remittances and Household Consumption Instability in Developing Countries. *World Development*. 39 (7). pp. 1076–89.

Combes, J.-L., C. Ebeke, S. Etoundi, and T. Yogo. 2014. Are Remittances and Foreign Aid a Hedge Against Food Price Shocks in Developing Countries? *World Development*. 54. pp. 81–98.

Cornia, G. A. 2016. An Econometric Analysis of the Bifurcation of Within-Country Inequality Trends in Sub-Saharan Africa, 1990–2011. *Africa Report*. 267781. New York: United Nations Development Programme.

Cornia, A. and S. Kiiski. 2002. Trends in Income Distribution Period: Evidence and Interpretation. *Wider Working Paper*. 2001. Helsinki: World Institute for Development Economics Research.

Costa, F., J. Garred, and J. P. Pessoa. 2016. Winners and Losers from a Commodities-for-Manufactures Trade Boom. *Journal of International Economics*. 102. pp. 50–69.

Costinot, A. and A. Rodríguez–Clare. 2014. Trade Theory with Numbers: Quantifying the Consequences of Globalization. In G. Gopinath, E. Helpman, and K. Rogoff (eds.). *Handbook of International Economics*. 4. Amsterdam: Elsevier.

Costinot, A. and J. Vogel. 2010. Matching and Inequality in the World Economy. *Journal of Political Economy*. 118 (4). pp. 747–86.

Crozet, M., T. Mayer, and J. J. Mucchielli. 2004. How Do Firms Agglomerate? A Study of FDI in France. *Regional Science and Urban Economics*. 34. pp. 27–54.

Cruz, M., G. Nayyar, G. Toews, and P.-L. Vézina. 2018. FDI and the Skill Premium: Evidence from Emerging Economies. *Policy Research Working Paper*. 8613. Washington, DC: World Bank.

Danzer, A.M., C. Feuerbaum, and F. Gaessler. 2020. Labor Supply and Automation Innovation. *IZA Discussion Paper*. 13429. Bonn: Institute for the Study of Labour.

Davies, S. <u>Remittances as Insurance for Household and Community Shocks in an Agricultural Economy: The Case of Rural Malawi</u>. Unpublished.

Davis, S. and T. von Watcher. 2011. Recessions and the Costs of Job Loss. *NBER Working Paper*. 17638. Cambridge, MA: National Bureau of Economic Research.

De Brauw, A., V. Mueller, and T. Woldehanna. 2013. Motives to Remit: Evidence from Tracked Internal Migrants in Ethiopia. *World Development*. 50. pp. 13–23.

De Haas, H., S. Fransen, et al. 2018. Social Transformation and Migration: An Empirical Inquiry. *International Migration Institute Network Working Paper*. 141. Amsterdam: International Migration Institute, Amsterdam Institute for Social Science Research, University of Amsterdam.

De Loecker, J. 2013. Detecting Learning by Exporting. *American Economic Journal: Microeconomics*. 5.

De Loecker, J. and P. Goldberg. 2014. Firm Performance in a Global Market. *Annual Review of Economics*. 6. pp. 201–27.

Dinga, M. and D. Münich. 2010. The Impact of Territorially Concentrated FDI on Local Labor Markets: Evidence from the Czech Republic. *Labour Economics.* 17 (2). pp. 354–67.

Dix-Carneiro, R. and B. Kovak. 2015. Trade Liberalization and the Skill Premium: A Local Labor Markets Approach. *American Economic Review.* 105 (5). pp. 551–57.

Dix-Carneiro, R. and B. Kovak. 2017. Trade Liberalization and Regional Dynamics. *American Economic Review.* 107 (10). pp. 2908–46.

Dix-Carneiro, R., R. R. Soares, and G. Ulyssea. 2018. Economic Shocks and Crime: Evidence from the Brazilian Trade Liberalization. *American Economic Journal: Applied Economics.* 10 (4). pp. 158–95.

Dollar, D. and A. Kraay. 2004. Trade, Growth, and Poverty. *The Economic Journal.* 114. pp.F22–F49.

Dollar, D., T. Kleineberg, and A. Kraay. 2016. Growth Still Is Good for the Poor. *European Economic Review.* 81.

Driffield, N. and M. Munday. 2000. Industrial Performance, Agglomeration, and Foreign Manufacturing Investment. *Journal of International Business Studies.* 31 (1). pp. 21–37.

Duggan, Victor, S. Rahardja, and G. Varela. 2013. Service Sector Reform and Manufacturing Productivity: Evidence from Indonesia. *Policy Research Working Paper Series.* 6349. Washington, DC: World Bank.

Dutt, P., D. Mitra, and P. Ranjan. 2009. International Trade and Unemployment: Theory and Cross-National Evidence. *Journal of International Economics.* 78.

Edmonds, E., N. Pavcnik, and P. Topalova. 2010. Trade Adjustment and Human Capital Investment: Evidence from Indian Tariff Reforms. *American Economic Journal: Applied Economics.* 2 (4). pp. 42–75.

Eichengreen, B., B. Csonto, A. El-Ganainy, and Z. Koczan. 2021. Financial Globalization and Inequality: Capital Flows as a Two-Edged Sword. *EBRD Working Paper.* 252. London: European Bank for Reconstruction and Development.

Erten, B. and J. Leight. 2017. Exporting Out of Agriculture: The Impact of WTO Accession on Structural Transformation in China. Mimeo.

Fagen, P. 2006. Remittances in Crises: A Haiti Case Study. *Humanitarian Policy Group Background Paper.* London: Overseas Development Institute.

Feenstra, R. C. and G. H. Hanson. 1997. Foreign Direct Investment and Relative Wages: Evidence from Mexico's Maquiladoras. *Journal of International Economics.* 42. pp. 371–93.

Felbermayr, G., J. Prat, and H. J. Schmerer. 2009. Trade and Unemployment: What Do the Data Say? *IZA Discussion Paper Series.* 4184. Bonn: Institute for the Study of Labour.

Figini, P. and H. Görg. 2011. Does Foreign Direct Investment Affect Wage Inequality? An Empirical Investigation. *IZA Discussion Paper Series.* 2336. Bonn: Institute for the Study of Labour.

Galbraith, J. K. and H. Kum. 2002. *Inequality and Economic and Econometric Tests.* Austin, TX: University of Texas, LBJ School of Public Inequality Project.

Giuliano, P. and A. Spilimbergo. 2009. Growing Up in a Recession: Beliefs and the Macroeconomy. *NBER Working Paper.* 15321. Cambridge, MA: National Bureau of Economic Research.

Goldberg, P. 2015. Review Article: Trade and Inequality. *Elgar Research Reviews in Economics.* Cheltenham, UK: Edward Elgar Publishing.

Goldberg, P. K. and N. Pavcnik. 2005. Trade, Wages, and the Political Economy of Trade Protection: Evidence from the Colombian Trade Reforms. *Journal of International Economics.* 66 (1). pp. 75–105.

Goldberg, P. and N. Pavcnik. 2007. Distributional Effects of Globalization in Developing Countries. *NBER Working Paper.* 12885. Cambridge, MA: National Bureau of Economic Research.

Goldberg, P. and N. Pavcnik. 2016. The Effects of Trade Policy. *NBER Working Paper.* 21957. Cambridge, MA: National Bureau of Economic Research.

Grogger, J. and G. H. Hanson. 2011. Income Maximization and the Selection and Sorting of International Migrants. *Journal of Development Economics.* 95 (1). pp. 42–57.

Gubert, F., T. Lassourd, and S. Mesple-Somps. 2010. Do Remittances Affect Poverty and Inequality? Evidence from Mali. *Document de Travail.* DT/2010–08. Paris: Université Paris-Dauphine.

Guimaraes, P., O. Figueiredo, and D. Woodward. 2000. Agglomeration and the Location of Direct Investment in Portugal. *Journal of Urban Economics.* 47. pp. 115–35.

Hale, G. and M. Xu. 2016. FDI Effects on the Labor Market of Host Countries. *Working Paper.* 2016-25. San Francisco, CA: Federal Reserve Bank of San Francisco.

Halliday, T. 2006. Migration, Risk and Liquidity Constraints in El Salvador. *Economic Development and Cultural Change.* 54. pp. 893–25.

Hallward-Driemeier, M. and G. Nayyar. 2017. *Trouble in the Making? The Future of Manufacturing-Led Development.* Washington, DC: World Bank.

Haque, S., M. Imamul, and I. A. Thaku. 2013. Role of Foreign Direct Investment in Labour Intensive Industries: A Comparison between India and China. *Global Journal of Commerce and Management Perspective.* 2 (3).

Harding, T. and B. S. Javorcik. 2011. Roll Out the Red Carpet and They Will Come: Investment Promotion and FDI Inflows. *Economic Journal*. 121 (557). pp. 1445–76.

Harding, T. and B. S. Javorcik. 2012. Foreign Direct Investment and Export Upgrading. *Review of Economics and Statistics*. 94 (4). pp. 964–80.

Hanson, G. and A. Harrison. 1999. Who Gains from Trade Reform? Some Remaining Puzzles. *Journal of Development Economics*. 59 (1). pp. 125–54.

Harrison, A. and A. Rodríguez-Clare. 2010. Trade, Foreign Investment, and Industrial Policy for Developing Countries. In D. Rodrik and M. R. Rosenzweig (eds.). *Handbook of Development Economics*. 5. Amsterdam: Elsevier. pp. 4039–214.

Hausmann, R., J. Hwang, and D. Rodrik. 2007. What You Export Matters. *Journal of Economic Growth*. 12 (1), pp. 1–25.

Head, K. and J. Ries. 2002. Offshore Production and Skill Upgrading by Japanese Manufacturing Firms. *Journal of International Economics*. 58. pp. 81–105.

Head, K., J. Ries, and D. L. Swenson. 1999. Attracting Foreign Manufacturing: Investment Promotion and Agglomeration. *Regional Science and Urban Economics*. 29. pp. 197–218.

Helpman, E., O. Itskhoki, and S. Redding. 2010. Inequality and Unemployment in a Global Economy. *Econometrica*. 78 (4). pp. 1239–83.

Helpman, E., O. Itskhoki, M. A. Muendler, and S. Redding. 2017. Trade and Inequality: From Theory to Estimation. *The Review of Economic Studies*. 84 (1). pp. 357–405.

Hinloopen, J. and C. Marrewijk. No date. Factor Intensity Classification.

International Monetary Fund. 2016. Spillovers from China's Transition and from Migration. *World Economic Outlook*. Washington, DC.

International Monetary Fund, World Bank, and World Trade Organization. 2018. *Reinvigorating Trade and Inclusive Growth*. Washington, DC: World Bank Group.

Javorcik, B. S. 2004. Does Foreign Direct Investment Increase the Productivity of Domestic Firms? In Search of Spillovers through Backward Linkages. *American Economic Review*. 94 (3). pp. 605–27.

Javorcik, B. S. 2014. Does FDI Bring Good Jobs to Host Countries? *Policy Research Working Paper*. 6936. Washington, DC: World Bank.

Javorcik, B. S., A. Lo Turco, and D. Maggioni. 2018. New and Improved: Does FDI Boost Production Complexity in Host Countries? *The Economic Journal*. 128 (614). pp. 2507–37.

Jensen, R. 2012. Do Labor Market Opportunities Affect Young Women's Work and Family Decisions? Experimental Evidence from India. *Quarterly Journal of Economics.* 127 (2). pp. 753–92.

Karlsson, S., N. Lundin, F. Sjöholm, and P. He. 2009. Foreign Firms and Chinese Employment. *The World Economy.* 32 (1). pp. 178–201.

Kletzer, L. G. 2001. *Job Loss from Imports: Measuring the Costs.* Washington, DC: Institute for International Economics.

Koczan, Zs. and F. Loyola. 2018. How Do Migration and Remittances Affect Inequality? A Case Study of Mexico. *IMF Working Paper.* 18/136. Washington, DC: International Monetary Fund.

Koczan, Zs., G. Peri, M. Pinat, and D. L. Rozhkov. 2021. The Impact of International Migration on Inclusive Growth: A Review. *IMF Working Paper.* 2021/088. Washington, DC: International Monetary Fund.

Kodama, N., B. S. Javorcik, and Y. Abe. 2018. Transplanting Corporate Culture Across International Borders: Foreign Direct Investment and Female Employment in Japan. *The World Economy.* 41 (5). pp. 1148–65.

Krugman, P. 1981. Intraindustry Specialization and the Gains from Trade. *Journal of Political Economy.* 89 (5). pp. 959–73.

Leamer, E. E. 1998. In Search of Stolper-Samuelson Effects on US Wages. In S. M. Collins (ed.). *Exports, Imports and the American Worker.* Washington, DC: Brookings Institution Press.

Lee, J. W. and D. Wie. 2015. Technological Change, Skill Demand, and Wage Inequality: Evidence from Indonesia. *World Development.* 67. pp. 238–50.

Lileeva, A. and D. Trefler. 2010. Improved Access to Foreign Markets Raises Plant-Level Productivity...For Some Plants. *The Quarterly Journal of Economics.* 125.

Lumenga-Neso, O., M. Olarreaga, and M. Schiff. 2005. On "Indirect" Trade-Related R&D Spillovers. *European Economic Review.* 49.

Lundberg, M. and L. Squire. 1999. *Growth and Inequality: Makers.* Washington, DC: World Bank.

Luo, R. 2017. Skill Premium and Technological Change in the Very Long Run: 1300–1914. *Discussion Papers in Economics.* 17/09. United Kingdom: University of Leicester.

Lustig, N. and R. Kanbur. 1999. Why Is Inequality Back on the Agenda? Paper prepared for the Annual World Bank Conference on Development Economics, Washington, DC. 28–30 April.

Margolis, D., L. Miotti, E. M. Mouhoud, and J. Oudinet. 2013. To Have and Have Not: Migration, Remittances, Poverty and Inequality in Algeria. *IZA Discussion Paper.* 7747. Bonn: Institute for the Study of Labour.

McCaig, B. 2011. Exporting Out of Poverty: Provincial Poverty in Vietnam and US Market Access. *Journal of International Economics*. 85 (1). pp. 102–13.

McLaren, J. and M. Yoo. 2016. FDI and Inequality in Vietnam: An Approach with Census Data. *NBER Working Paper*. 22930. Cambridge, MA: National Bureau of Economic Research.

Melitz, M. 2003. The Impact of Trade on Intra-Industry Reallocations and Aggregate Industry Productivity. *Econometrica*. 71 (6). pp. 1695–725.

Melitz, M. J. and S. J. Redding. 2014. Heterogeneous Firms and Trade. In G. Gopinath, E. Helpman, and K. Rogoff (eds.). *Handbook of International Economics*. 4. Amsterdam: Elsevier. pp. 1–54.

Meschi, E. and M. Vivarelli. 2009. Trade and Income Inequality in Developing Countries. *World Development*. 37 (2). pp. 287–302.

Mihaylova, S. 2015. Foreign Direct Investment and Income Inequality in Central and Eastern Europe. *Theoretical and Applied Economics*. 22, (2 [603]). pp. 23–42.

Milanovic, B. 2005. Can We Discern the Effect of Globalization on Income Distribution? Evidence from Household Surveys. *The World Bank Economic Review*. 19 (1). pp. 21–44.

Mohapatra, S., G. Joseph, and D. Ratha. 2009. Remittances and Natural Disasters: Ex-Post Response and Contribution to Ex-Ante Preparedness. *Policy Research Working Paper*. 4972. Washington, DC: World Bank.

Möllers, J. and W. Meyer. 2014. The Effects of Migration on Poverty and Inequality in Rural Kosovo. *IZA Journal of Labor & Development*. 3 (16).

Mughal, M. and A. I. Anwar. 2012. Remittances, Inequality and Poverty in Pakistan: Macro and Microeconomic Evidence. *CATT Working Paper*. 2. Cedex, France: Centre d'Analyse Théorique et de Traitement des données économiques.

Notowidigdo, M. J. 2013. The Incidence of Local Labor Demand Shocks. *NBER Working Paper*. 17167. Cambridge, MA: National Bureau of Economic Research.

Nunnenkamp, P., R. Schweickert, and M. Wiebelt. 2007. Distributional Effects of FDI: How the Interaction of FDI and Economic Policy Affects Poor Households in Bolivia. *Development Policy Review*. 25 (4). pp. 429–50.

Organisation for Economic Co-operation and Development (OECD). 2005. Trade-Adjustment Costs in OECD Labour Markets: A Mountain or a Molehill? *OECD Employment Outlook*. Paris: OECD.

OECD. 2012. *Trade, Growth and Jobs. Summary of the OECD and International Collaborative Initiative on Trade and Employment Report on Policy Priorities for International Trade and Jobs*. Paris: OECD.

OECD. 2017. *Interrelations between Public Policies, Migration and Development.* Paris: OECD.

Ohlin, B. 1933. *Interregional and International Trade.* Cambridge, MA: Harvard University Press.

Olney, W. W. and D. Pozzoli. 2021. The Impact of Immigration on Firm-Level Offshoring. *The Review of Economics and Statistics.* 103 (1). pp. 177–95.

Oreopoulos, P., M. Page, and A. H. Stevens. 2008. The Intergenerational Effects of Worker Displacement. *Journal of Labour Economics.* 26 (3). pp. 455–83.

Ortega, F. and G. Peri. 2013. The Effect of Income and Immigration Policies on International Migration. *Migration Studies.* 1 (1). pp. 47–74.

Oster, E. and B. Steinberg. 2013. Do IT Service Centers Promote School Enrollment? Evidence from India. *Journal of Development Economics.* 104. p. 123–35.

Parsons, C. and P. Vezina. Forthcoming. Migrant Networks and Trade: The Vietnamese Boat People as a Natural Experiment. *The Economic Journal.*

Pavcik, N. 2017. The Impact of Trade on Inequality in Developing Countries. *NBER Working Paper.* 23878. Cambridge, MA: National Bureau of Economic Research.

Peluffo, A. 2015. Foreign Direct Investment, Productivity, Demand for Skilled Labour and Wage Inequality: An Analysis of Uruguay. *World Economy.* 38 (6). pp. 962–83.

Perea, J. R. and M. Stephenson. 2018. Outward FDI from Developing Countries. *Global Investment Competitiveness Report 2017/2018.* Washington, DC: World Bank Group. pp. 101–34.

Pierce, J. R. and P. K. Schott. 2016a. The Surprisingly Swift Decline of US Manufacturing Employment. *American Economic Review.* 106 (7). pp. 1632–62.

Pierce, J. R. and P. K. Schott. 2016b. Trade Liberalization and Mortality: Evidence from US Counties. *NBER Working Paper.* 22849. Cambridge, MA: National Bureau of Economic Research.

Qiang, C. Z. and P. Kusek. 2020. Overview. *Global Investment Competitiveness Report 2019/2020.* Washington, DC: World Bank.

Ravallion, M. 2001. Growth, Inequality, and Poverty: Looking Beyond Averages. *World Development.* 29 (11). pp. 1803-1815.

Ricardo, D. 1817. *On the Principles of Political Economy and Taxation.* First edition. London: John Murray.

Robertson, Raymond. 2000. Trade Liberalisation and Wage Inequality: Experience. *World Economy.* 23 (6). pp. 827–49.

Rodrik, D. 2006a. Industrial Development: Stylized Facts and Policies. Draft. Unpublished.

Rodrik, D. 2006b. What's So Special about China's Exports? *China & World Economy*. 14 (5). pp. 1–19.

Samuelson, P. 1939. The Gains from International Trade. *Canadian Journal of Economics and Political Science*. 5. pp. 195–205.

Stark, O., J. Edward Taylor, and S. Yitzhaki. 1988. Migration, Remittances and Inequality: A Sensitivity Analysis Using the Extended Gini Index. *Journal of Development Economics*. 28. pp. 309–22.

Suleri, A. Q. and K. Savage. 2006. Remittances in Crises: A Case Study from Pakistan. *Humanitarian Policy Group Background Paper*. London: Overseas Development Institute.

Taylor, J. E., R. Adams, J. Mora, and A. López-Feldman. 2005. *Remittances, Inequality and Poverty: Evidence from Rural Mexico*. *Working Paper*. 05-003. Davis, CA: Department of Agricultural and Resource Economics, University of California.

Te Velde, D. W. and T. Xenogiani. 2007. Foreign Direct Investment and International Skill Inequality. *Oxford Development Studies*. 35 (1). pp. 83–104.

Topalova, P. 2007. Trade Liberalization, Poverty and Inequality: Evidence from Indian Districts. In A. Harrison (ed.). *Globalization and Poverty*. Chicago, IL: University of Chicago Press.

Topalova, P. 2010. Factor Immobility and Regional Impacts of Trade Liberalization: Evidence on Poverty from India. *American Economic Journal: Applied Economics*. 2 (4). pp. 1–41.

Waldkirch, A., P. Nunnenkamp, and J. E. Alatorre Bremont. 2009. Employment Effects of FDI in Mexico's Non-Maquiladora Manufacturing. *Journal of Development Studies*. 45 (7). pp. 1165–83.

Woodward, D. P. 1992. Locational Determinants of Japanese Manufacturing Start-Ups in the United States. *Southern Journal of Economics*. 53. pp. 690–708.

World Bank. 2006. *Global Economic Prospects: Economic Implications of Remittances and Migration*. Washington, DC.

World Bank. 2020. *Global Investment Competitiveness Report 2019/2020*. Washington, DC.

Wu, T. 2006. The Role of Remittances in Crisis: An Aceh Research Study. *Humanitarian Policy Group Background Paper*. London: Overseas Development Institute.

Yang, D. and C. Martinez. 2005. Remittances and Poverty in Migrants' Home Areas: Evidence from the Philippines. Unpublished.

5 Regional Approaches to Support Air Pollution Management in South Asia

To ensure the provision of regional public goods, a deep understanding and appreciation of complex, technical, and economic dimensions of major development issues is needed. In South Asia, the regional airshed approach indicates that the most cost-effective solution for the whole region is a regionally coordinated one.

Background

The health impacts of air pollution are a major impetus to air pollution control policies all over the world.[20] Air pollution exposure was the cause of 11.3% of all female deaths and 12.2% of all male deaths globally in 2019, accounting for 6.67 million deaths (Murray et al. 2020). Fine particulate matter 2.5 microns or less in diameter ($PM_{2.5}$) has been linked to premature mortality and morbidity associated with ischemic heart disease, stroke, chronic obstructive lung disease, lower respiratory infections, type 2 diabetes, and lung cancer. Air pollution exposure has been associated with premature birth and low birthweight and childhood asthma. Studies have found that $PM_{2.5}$ enters the brain of young children and can affect cognitive development and intelligence quotients. The impacts of air pollution exposure on dementia have been established.

South Asia is the epicenter of the continuing threat to public health from ambient (outdoor) air pollution. According to recent Global Burden of Disease Study estimates (*The Lancet 2020*), air pollution contributes to about 17% of all deaths in South Asia. Nearly 95% of South Asians live where ambient $PM_{2.5}$ exceeds the World Health Organization (WHO) Air Quality Guideline of an annual mean of 10 micrograms per cubic meter ($\mu g/m^3$). Almost 60% live where fine particulate matter exceeds even the least stringent WHO interim air quality target of an annual mean of 35 $\mu g/m^3$ (World Bank 2021). Detailed country-by-country results are shown in Table 8.

Ambient air pollution is especially severe in fast-growing urban regions, where the combination of denser population, more motorized vehicles and construction activity, uncontrolled solid waste burning, and use of polluting energy sources results in elevated pollutant levels and human exposure. Of the top 20 cities in the world with the poorest air quality in 2016, 17 were in South Asia (Figure 29).

The health effects of air pollution have significant economic impacts. Premature deaths associated with air pollution reduce human capital, cutting short the output that people would have contributed to the economy had they lived (Table 9). Air pollution–related morbidity reduces economic output because people are unable to work and because they are less productive

---

[20] This chapter is based on the forthcoming World Bank report *Striving for Clean Air: Air Pollution and Public Health in South Asia*. In producing this report, the World Bank emphasizes that air pollution–related and projects shall respect the sovereignty of the countries involved, and notes that the findings and conclusions in the report may not reflect the views of individual countries or their acceptance.

when they can work (Chang et al. 2019). The annual cost of health damages in South Asian countries is estimated at 1.5%–10.6% of gross domestic product (GDP) equivalent (World Bank 2021).[21]

Table 8: Premature Mortality Attributable to Ambient Air Pollution and Household Air Pollution in South Asia

Country	Premature Mortality Attributable Risk		
	AAP (PM$_{2.5}$ + ground-level ozone) (Deaths)	HAP (Deaths)	Total Burden (Deaths)
Afghanistan	9,154	28,168	36,847
Bangladesh	104,725	94,789	168,785
Bhutan	335	352	621
India	1,147,669	606,890	1,586,571
Maldives	59	23	72
Nepal	23,974	21,603	39,552
Pakistan	124,912	116,090	230,098
Sri Lanka	7,538	6,643	13,904
South Asia	**1,285,522**	**94,789**	**1,662,970**

AAP = ambient air pollution, HAP = household air pollution, PM = particulate matter.

Note: The risks caused by exposure to AAP and HAP. For example, given that the sum of AAP-related deaths in India (1,147,669) and HAP-related deaths (606,890) is about 168,000 greater than the total (1,586,571) number of deaths attributable to air pollution risk, the 168,000 premature deaths may be associated with exposure to both HAP and AAP (i.e., cases of heart attack, stroke, pneumonia, or cancer, where a patient was exposed to both forms of pollution).

Source: The Lancet. 2020. *Global Burden of Disease Study 2019*.

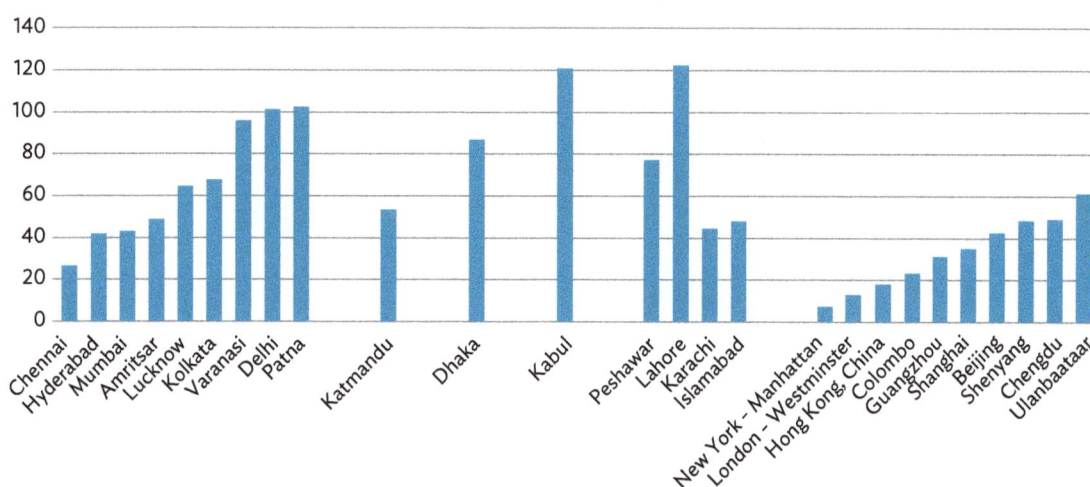

Figure 29: Top 20 Most Polluted Cities in the World: 17 in South Asia

Source: Calculations from 2019 air quality data from OpenAQ and AirNow.

---

[21]   These measures of economic output losses do not include important costs to human well-being that are not measured in national accounts. For example, illness causes a loss of well-being beyond lost wages and costs of medical care. People who are ill know that illnesses caused by air pollution shorten life, and that awareness diminishes their well-being. The World Bank and the Institute for Health Metrics and Evaluation (2016) thoroughly discuss the categories of social cost caused by air pollution and their measurement.

Table 9: Cost of Health Damages in South Asia

Country	Cost of Health Damages ($ million)			Gross Domestic Product Equivalent
	AAP	HAP	Total	
Afghanistan	312	1,047	1,359	7.1%
Bangladesh	11,173	15,365	26,538	8.8%
Bhutan	94	125	219	8.5%
India	184,291	121,397	305,689	10.6%
Maldives	59	28	87	1.5%
Nepal	1,398	1,723	3,121	10.2%
Pakistan	11,943	12,845	24,788	8.9%
Sri Lanka	3,380	3,401	6,781	8.1%
	212,650	155,931	368,582	

AAP = ambient air pollution, HAP = household air pollution.
Source: World Bank (2021).

Reducing ambient air pollution has important co-benefits. Vigorous clean air policies have non-health–related benefits as they can mitigate greenhouse gas (GHG) emissions.[22] A general-equilibrium effect not included in the figures above is that cities that pursue stronger mitigation policies become more attractive to more highly skilled workers, which may spur overall growth by strengthening agglomeration effects.

Air Quality Management in South Asia

South Asian countries have made strides in strengthening air quality management (AQM) programs but need to do more. Recent years have seen a wave of policy responses to combat air pollution, including the Draft Bangladesh Clean Air Act, the National Electrical Vehicles Policy in Pakistan, and India's National Clean Air Programme. The policy changes will allow economies to grow without a corresponding increase in air pollution. However, beyond these decoupling efforts, further measures beyond the current policies are needed to reduce particulate pollution to a level meeting WHO's first interim target for $PM_{2.5}$ emissions (annual mean exposure of 35 μg/m³).

The diversity of pollutant sources and locations underscores the complexity of air pollution. Much of the focus of air pollution management has been on city air pollution, looking at specific stationary or mobile sources in a certain geographic area or within political boundaries, such as a city or municipality. However, air pollution is transported long distances across boundaries and is often a function of wind climatology and cloud chemistry. Figure 30, which shows the results of a recent assessment of fine particulate sources in Delhi, indicates the variety of sources (including agricultural activities and industry and power plants) and significant contributions from outside Delhi (Amann et al. 2016).

---

[22]   All countries in South Asia have submitted nationally determined contributions as a part of 2015 Paris Climate Agreement, indicating the levels to which they will reduce their GHG emissions.

Figure 30: Sector and Spatial Origin of PM$_{2.5}$ in Ambient Air in Delhi National Capital Territory, 2018

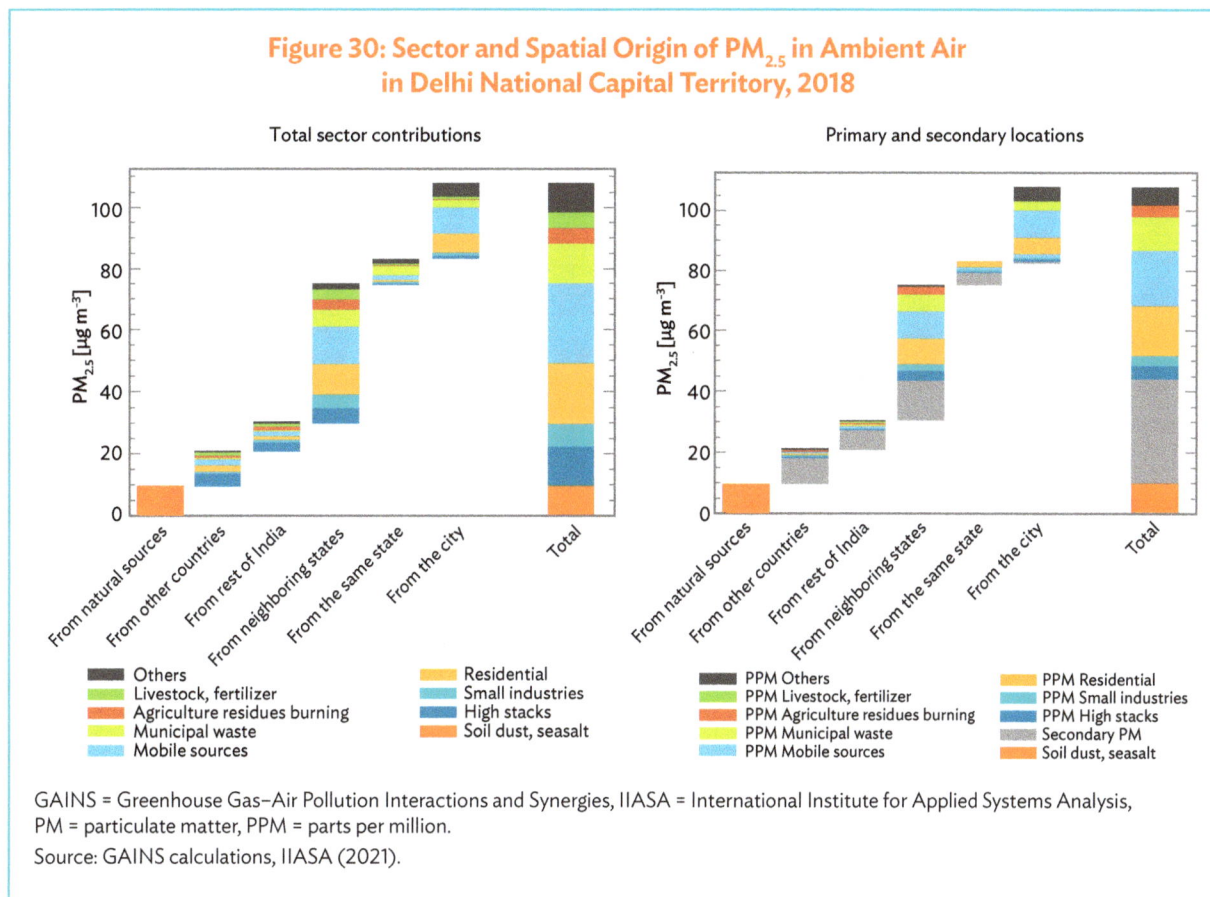

GAINS = Greenhouse Gas–Air Pollution Interactions and Synergies, IIASA = International Institute for Applied Systems Analysis, PM = particulate matter, PPM = parts per million.

Source: GAINS calculations, IIASA (2021).

From a policy perspective, therefore, it makes sense to identify and characterize airsheds to better understand the sources and impacts of air pollution and formulate responses instead of confining responses within political boundaries (Box 9). Regional management of air pollution is even more important than that of water pollution because the effects of air pollution more commonly cross political jurisdictions.

Multilateral development banks (MDBs) and national finance institutions have long supported AQM programs, especially those that result in tangible health benefits. Although South Asian countries have already taken concrete steps to reduce emissions and improve air quality, innovative financing, especially to link payments to performance—such as improved ambient air quality and emission reductions based on set targets—to increase commercial sector engagement, will only accelerate the pace of the policy changes. The air quality program of India's Fifteenth Finance Commission (2021–2026), which uses devolved tax revenues, is another example of a large-scale innovative financial initiative that links payments to achieving air quality improvement targets for large cities.

The research here provides new insights to help air quality policy makers better assess the environmental effectiveness of policy measures and the circumstances in which cross-jurisdictional cooperation is necessary. The Greenhouse Gas–Air Pollution Interactions and Synergies (GAINS) methodology used here is described in the Annex. While information

Box 9: Regional Airshed Approaches to Dealing with Air Pollution

An airshed can be defined as a geographic area that, because of topography, meteorology, and/or climate, is frequently affected by the same air mass. Consequently, air quality within the airshed depends on pollution sources in it but not outside it. Airsheds can vary in size, from small areas in valleys to urban-scale and even region-wide airsheds, where the effects of air pollution may extend over hundreds of kilometers. An airshed may have areas where pollution levels are elevated because of individual or a group of emission sources, such as one or two polluting industries or proximity to a congested roadway. The wind can move pollution large distances, so some form of subjective judgment is needed to determine how much cross-boundary transfer is acceptable before the airshed boundary needs to be extended.

The concept of an airshed as a planning and management tool is analogous to the idea of a watershed or drainage basin in water resources. Fundamental differences, however, exist between them. Unlike water pollution, air pollution is more demanding to sample as it comes from a variety of nonpoint sources.

Many countries consider the airshed a policy tool. The United States (US) established 247 airsheds under the 1970 Clean Air Act, which formed the basis for air pollution control policies. Airsheds were classified according to whether they attained the National Ambient Air Quality Standards, and whether pollution control measures had been implemented to attain them.

In New Zealand, implementing the National Environmental Standards is linked to establishing airsheds or local air quality management areas for the entire country. Detailed methodological criteria are used to define attainment levels of areas vis-à-vis national standards. The country has 72 airsheds.

Airsheds have been a policy tool in the Philippines since 2005. The Philippine Clean Air Act and its implementing rules and regulations require designation of airsheds to manage air quality and protect public health. As in the US, airsheds that meet the national air quality value for criteria pollutants are declared attainment areas, while those that exceed the standards or do not comply with them are labeled non-attainment areas.

The People's Republic of China (PRC), too, is moving to a regional approach to deal with its huge air pollution problem. For example, the PRC pays greater attention to regional agglomerations such as the Beijing–Tianjin–Hebei region. The reason is that, although Beijing had invested significant efforts and resources in air pollution control since the late 1990s, the city's air quality continued to worsen because of rapid development of heavily polluting industries in surrounding provinces. Therefore, the Beijing–Tianjin–Hebei region adopted a joint air pollution control strategy in 2013, covering 13 cities in Greater Beijing. Given the success of the regional approach in reducing pollution, the cluster approach has been scaled up to cover many cities across the PRC. PRC studies show that the three major city clusters (the Beijing–Tianjin–Hebei region and the Yangtze and Pearl river deltas) suffer from severe transboundary air pollution.

India's recent National Clean Air Programme calls for a regional approach to dealing with air pollution, including by establishing regional coordination mechanisms. It states, "...since air pollution is not a localized phenomenon, the effect is felt in cities and towns far away from the source thus creating the need of inter-state and inert-city coordination in addition to multisectoral synchronization."

Source: Author.

about the concentration of ambient air pollution in particular locations is admittedly imperfect, the concentrations are the result of emissions from many different sources in different locations. Concentrations depend on such factors as weather and topography. The objective, therefore, is to identify workable definitions of airsheds in South Asia that can be used to evaluate air quality policy options, and then to measure the level and composition of air pollution concentration in them.

Sources of Pollution

As in many other regions, power generation, large industries, and mobile sources are responsible for significant levels of total $PM_{2.5}$ concentrations in South Asia, together often exceeding WHO guideline values. However, other sources that are less important in other regions substantially add to the pollution load in South Asia. The sources include, among others, residential solid fuel combustion (e.g., for cooking); small industries (e.g., brick kilns) burning high-emission solid fuels; current management practices of municipal waste (including plastic burning); and inefficient application of mineral fertilizer, fireworks, and cremation.

Because of the diverse sources of $PM_{2.5}$ in ambient air in South Asia, particulate matter at any given receptor site traces back to many sectors. While quantitative shares differ across cities and regions because of local topographic, meteorological, and economic factors, except for isolated pollution hot spots, no single sector can be identified as the single source responsible for most $PM_{2.5}$ at any given location (Figure 31).

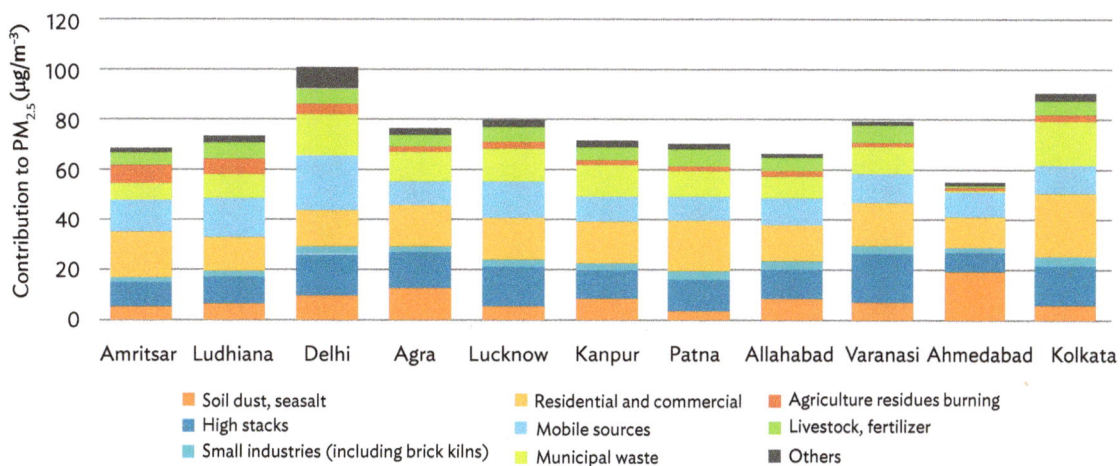

Figure 31: Contributions of Source Sectors to Population-Weighted $PM_{2.5}$ Exposure in Major Cities in the Indo-Gangetic Plain, 2018

GAINS = Greenhouse Gas–Air Pollution Interactions and Synergies, IIASA = International Institute for Applied Systems Analysis, PM = particulate matter.
Source: GAINS calculations, IIASA (2021).

Figure 32: Contributions of Source Sectors to Population-Weighted PM$_{2.5}$ Exposure in Major Cities Outside the Indo-Gangetic Plain, 2018

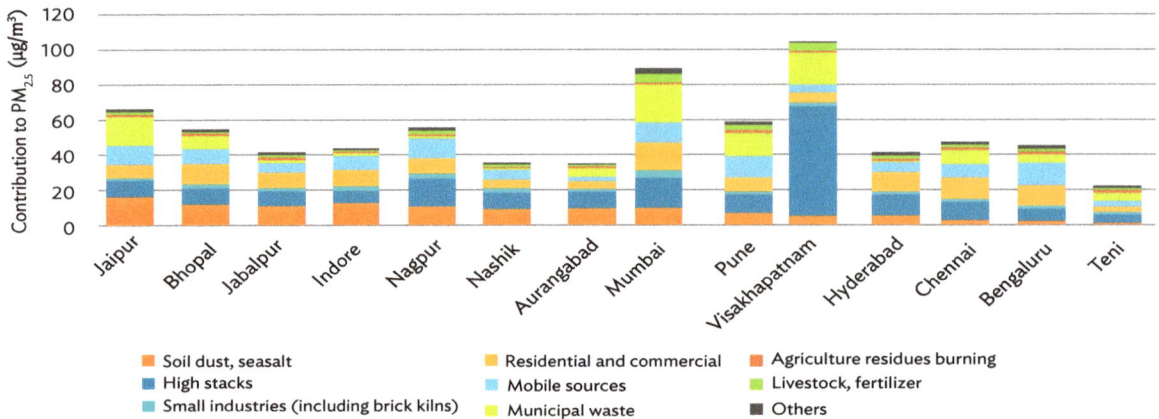

GAINS = Greenhouse Gas–Air Pollution Interactions and Synergies, IIASA = International Institute for Applied Systems Analysis, PM = particulate matter.

Source: GAINS calculations, IIASA (2021).

Figure 33: Contributions of Source Sectors to Population-Weighted PM$_{2.5}$ Exposure in Major Cities in Other South Asian Countries, 2018

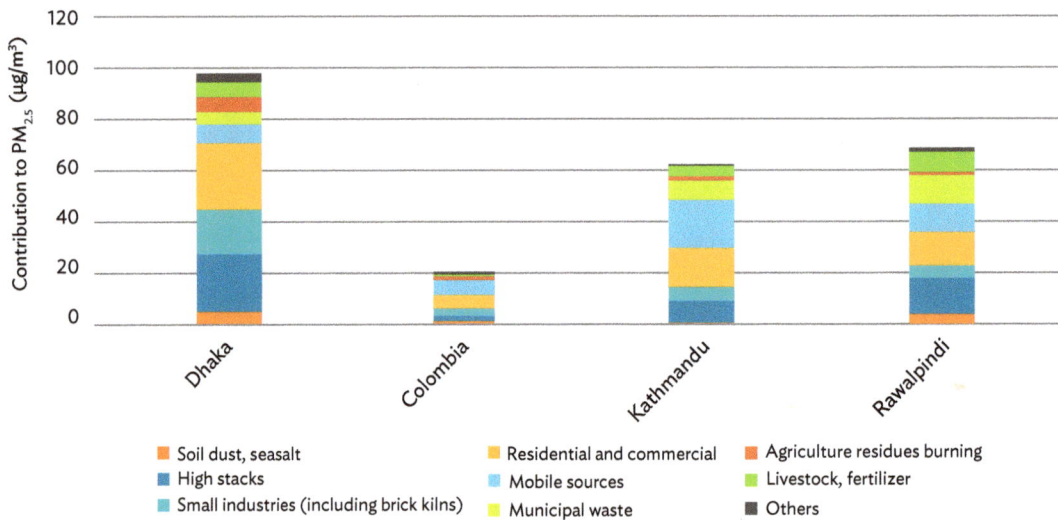

GAINS = Greenhouse Gas–Air Pollution Interactions and Synergies, IIASA = International Institute for Applied Systems Analysis, PM = particulate matter.

Source: GAINS calculations, IIASA (2021).

Because of the multisector character of sources of air pollution in South Asia, effective AQM must involve, in addition to sources that past efforts focused on (road transport and large point sources), other sectors that are important in specific subregions, such as household energy uses, small industries, waste management, and agricultural activities.

Based on the insights presented here, the research explores alternative AQM options that could improve air quality and bring population exposure closer to international air quality standards.

Strategy Going Forward

Population growth, progressing urbanization, and economic development, combined with the impacts of recent emission control legislation, will change the relative importance of various economic sectors to the population's exposure, as well as pollution transport between cities, surrounding states, neighboring regions, and other countries in South Asia.

The research develops a baseline projection for 2030, revealing the pivotal importance of full implementation and enforcement of the recently adopted air quality legislation. Based on four pollution control scenarios, the research explores the cost-effectiveness of alternative approaches for further air quality improvement in South Asia and distills the implications for AQM planning.

Given the limited air quality improvements that can be expected from recent legislation, the research examines additional air quality and cost implications of four alternative approaches for AQM in South Asia. Four scenarios illustrate the implications of alternative AQM approaches that differ in ambition, rationales for prioritizing efforts, and degree of coordination across jurisdictions. Beyond the measures prescribed in the 2018 legislation in each region, additional emission controls are chosen in 2030 according to the following:

- An **ad hoc selection of measures** scenario assesses upscaling the measures being implemented in parts of South Asia to the whole region. Following widespread thinking in the region, the focus is on the power sector, large industries, and road transport. Cost-effectiveness of improving air quality receives less attention and measures are often decided regardless of air quality interactions with other territories.

- For reference, a second **maximum technically feasible emission reduction** scenario explores the range of air quality improvements that could be achieved in 2030 by fully implementing all technical emission controls that are available on the world market, irrespective of costs. However, excluding premature scrapping of existing capital stock, new technologies are implemented only with new investments.

- As a more targeted approach, AQM could focus on pollution hot spots in South Asia and bring mean population exposure to $PM_{2.5}$ in each region to **comply with the first interim target of the World Health Organization** ($35\,\mu g/m^3$). Where the mitigation of long-range transport of pollution to the most polluted areas requires regional coordination, measures in other regions are selected based on their cost-effectiveness.

- Finally, a fourth option seeks cost-effective cuts of harmful population exposure to PM$_{2.5}$ through a common but differentiated approach coordinated across South Asia. With a long-term perspective of **moving to the next-lower WHO interim target for PM$_{2.5}$** (i.e., 10 µg/m³), governments select measures so that by 2030 the mean population exposure in each region falls below the next-lower WHO interim target compared with 2018 (35, 25, and 15 µg/m³). Governments choose measures based on their cost-effectiveness and, where necessary, coordinate with neighboring regions. The scenario can be contrasted with the "compliance scenario" in that the measures considered will be less stringent and the WHO interim target will not necessarily be achieved in all areas.

Figure 34: Exposure Reductions and Associated Emission Control Costs of the Four Emission Control Scenarios

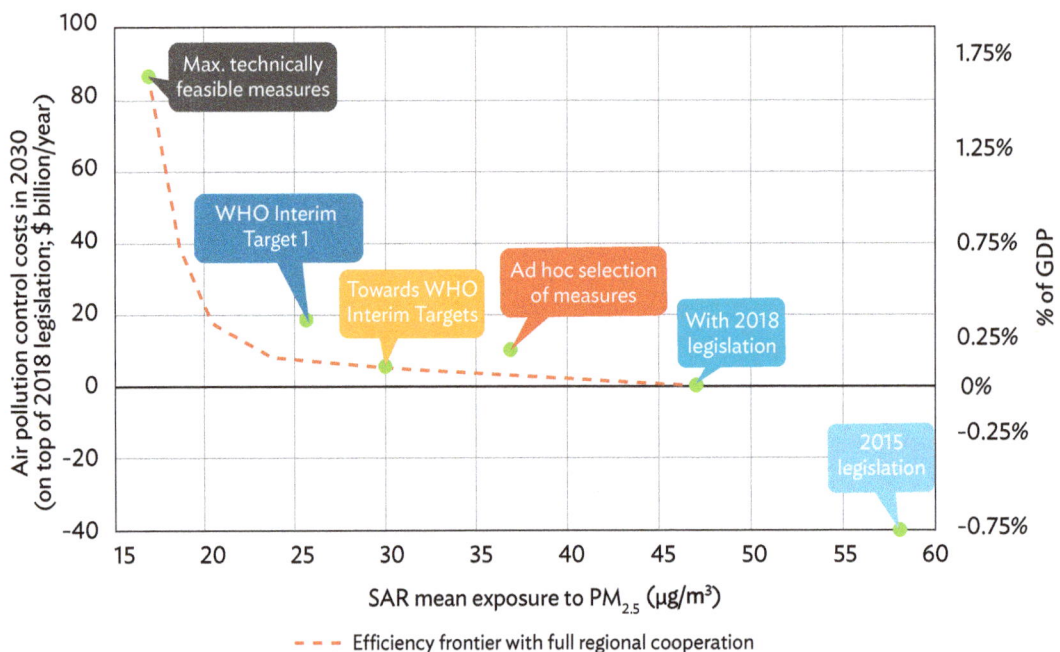

GDP = gross domestic product, PM = particulate matter, SAR = South Asia region, WHO = World Health Organization.
Source: Author.

The four AQM approaches differ not only in quantity and regional distribution of exposure improvement but also in cost-effectiveness, i.e., costs to reduce exposure by a certain amount. As a benchmark, compliance with the 2018 legislation involves about $74 billion per year in 2030, i.e., 1.4% of GDP, reducing mean population exposure to PM$_{2.5}$ in South Asia to about 47 µg/m³ in 2030, compared with 50.5 µg/m³ in 2018 (Figure 34).

Full implementation of all technically feasible emission controls would cut exposure to 17 µg/m³, i.e., by two-thirds compared with 2018, at additional emission control costs of $86 billion per year (1.6% of GDP) on top of the 2018 legislation, resulting in cost-effectiveness of $2,576 million per µg/m³ exposure reduction.

Upscaling current emission controls under the "ad hoc selection of measures" scenario would reduce mean exposure to 37 µg/m³ (i.e., by about one-quarter relative to 2018), at additional emission control costs (beyond those of the 2018 legislation) of $10.6 billion per year (0.20% of GDP in 2030).

In contrast, focusing on the most polluted areas by bringing down exposure everywhere below WHO's first interim target (35 µg/m³) doubles the decline of mean exposure in South Asia to 26 µg/m³ because of the co-benefits of upwind measures at other locations. Additional costs increase to $19 billion per year (0.35% of GDP). With about $780 million per µg/m³ exposure reductions, cost-effectiveness is similar in both approaches.

The most cost-effective air quality improvements emerge from a common but differentiated move to the WHO interim targets. If each region cuts exposure below the next-lower interim target, mean exposure in South Asia declines to 30 µg/m³, i.e., by 40% below 2018 levels. Additional costs amount to $5.7 billion per year, i.e., 0.11% of GDP. Notably, costs of such an approach are 45% lower than those of the "ad hoc selection of measures" strategy and will reduce total exposure in South Asia by 70% more. With $278 million per µg/m³ exposure reduction, the approach is the most cost-effective.

Cost-effectiveness emerges from tailored solutions that respond to the regional diversity of South Asia. The "toward WHO interim targets" scenario maximizes cost-effectiveness by identifying for each region the measures that deliver the differentiated exposure targets at least cost. Across South Asia, the baskets of priority measures show significant differences, reflecting the large diversity in economic structures, emission sources, topographic situations, population densities, meteorological conditions, already applied emission controls, and remaining potential for further measures.

Access to water and sanitation. Children cool off with clean, piped water in Khan village, Lao People's Democratic Republic (photo by ADB).

Conclusions

Cost-effective AQM requires airshed-wide coordination. The atmospheric transport of pollution not only demands coordination of response measures between states in areas with high emission densities, but also implies a need to extend the scope of current city-scale AQM practices in South Asia. Depending on among other things, the size of a city, in many urban agglomerations a dominant share of pollution can originate from outside sources.

Successful AQM depends on establishing mechanisms for cross-jurisdictional cooperation. Dependence on outside administrations responsible for outside emission sources creates demanding governance challenges for AQM. Around the world, many mechanisms have fostered constructive cooperation and delivered important public health and economic benefits. Measures taken within a region do not only improve air quality within the region but also deliver additional air quality benefits in downwind areas. Depending on the size of the source region, population densities, the topographic situation, and meteorological conditions, benefits occurring outside the region can exceed local benefits. Cost–benefit analyses need to account for the additional benefits, and the costs of delivering them, to establish mechanisms to realize shared benefits.

Cost-effectiveness can be balanced across regions to maximize cost savings and shared benefits from airshed-wide coordination. The strong mutual interconnections between pollution inflow from upwind sources and the outflow into downwind areas open AQM opportunities. To achieve the 2030 targets cost-effectively, each jurisdiction and country must cooperatively select measures and policies that have the greatest impact at the lowest cost. The GAINS model provides a scientific tool for systematic analyses that have proven effective in shaping cost-effective airshed policies in Europe and the PRC.

This research puts forward the "toward WHO targets" scenario as the most cost-effective path to get as close to WHO's first interim target as possible. Although governments must cooperate to realize favorable outcomes, progress to better air quality depends on persistent local investments.

Because of South Asia's diversity, portfolios of cost-effective measures and the relative importance of individual measures vary. While priority sectors are diverse, measures to reduce emissions from solid fuel use in households and from municipal waste management offer the largest potential. Because of the multisector character of air pollution sources, effective AQM must involve—in addition to sources that past efforts focused on (road transport and large point sources)—other sectors specific to the region: households, small industries, waste management, and agricultural activities.

Cross-jurisdictional cooperation among governments can evolve. Individual countries should continue to build up strong national AQM programs, then gradually expand intergovernmental cooperation on AQM technical challenges and policy designs. Countries must continue to progress to more protective ambient air quality standards to reach WHO's first interim target of 35 $\mu g/m^3$ (population-weighted average) by 2030. Further progress to WHO's second and third interim targets will follow, with the goal of achieving ambient $PM_{2.5}$ concentrations below 10$\mu g/m^3$.

The international experience is that, as countries move forward in AQM, the next step is applying cost-effectiveness after developing core environmental management skills (determining emission quantities, ambient air quality, air pollution sources, among others). Determining cost–benefit will require even further refined data and multisector analytical skills. Countries could work together to boost these development stages.

South Asia has been and continues to be heavily impacted by the coronavirus disease (COVID-19) pandemic. Regional growth is expected to contract by 7.7% in 2020, after exceeding 6.0% annually since 2015 (World Bank 2020). In 2021, regional growth is projected to rebound to 4.5%. However, factoring in population growth, per-capita income will remain 6% below 2019 figures, deepening poverty.

Countries have responded to the pandemic with health emergency measures, including lockdowns. Governments gave emergency financial and social support to the poor, households, and businesses. Central banks maintained financial stability.

The three largest government-supported emergency responses in the first 3 months of the pandemic were in India ($276.0 billion or 10% of GDP), Pakistan ($7.3 billion or 2.6% GDP), and Bangladesh ($11.8 billion or 3.6% of GDP). While the packages largely aimed to provide emergency support, a few activities were environmentally beneficial, such as Pakistan's green tsunami tree-planting program. Some activities, however, included support for activities that deepen dependence on fossil fuels and worsen climate change.

Supporting resilient recovery is the third stage of pandemic response. MDBs recognize three stages in pandemic response: (i) emergency support; (ii) restructuring of health, social, and economic systems; and (iii) support for resilient recovery, including by mitigating the existential threat of climate change.

As countries start to recover from the pandemic, they can either return to business as usual as rapidly as possible or review current expenditures and economic policies and build back better to become more efficient, pro-poor, sustainable, and resilient to future shocks, including from climate change. The resilient COVID-19 recovery approach is especially important as countries need to ensure that they make the right investment choices to emerge stronger after the pandemic. For instance, investing in expanding fossil fuels and older carbon-intensive technologies such as coal-fired power plants, which are being outbid by low-cost renewable energy and battery storage, would be a mistake. Fossil fuels and carbon-intensive technologies could become stranded assets—stranded physical assets and financial liabilities to investors—apart from being bad for the climate.

When South Asian countries started enforcing lockdowns to contain COVID-19, metropolises across the subregion recorded significantly lower levels of nitrogen dioxide and sulfur dioxide, both harmful chemicals released by motor vehicles and power plants. Cities with historically high concentration levels of particulate matter ($PM_{2.5}$) saw substantially reduced pollution, although further analysis is needed to determine whether natural sources or human activities explain the decrease. Despite the welcome respite, air pollution has long been a major public health threat in South Asia, representing the third-highest risk for premature death.

While lockdowns had the temporary side benefit of cleaner air and bluer skies, previous exposure to pollution has likely made more South Asians vulnerable to contracting severe respiratory diseases, including complications from COVID-19. A scientific consensus is emerging that improving air quality could play an important role in overcoming the pandemic. Although at an early stage, research implies that pollution must be limited as much as possible when lockdowns are lifted to minimize the impact of a second or a third wave of the coronavirus. The emerging findings offer an opportunity not only to enforce air pollution regulations to protect human health (during and after COVID-19) but also to ensure that we get out of the crisis with the prospect of less air pollution.

Countries can promote cleaner fuels and adopt more environment-friendly transport and energy technologies. For example, some cities in Europe are already planning to emerge from the lockdown with cleaner transport options in place.

MDBs can develop and use large-scale performance-based finance to bring together states, provinces, and divisions within and across countries to ensure that jurisdictions within delineated airsheds are working jointly to improve air quality that benefits the overall airshed.

Many MDBs can leverage the already pledged to scale financing for climate change programs and increase the integration of climate change into their development finance portfolios. AQM and climate change mitigation often go together, and South Asian countries can align with the new priorities. The next step is to define climate co-benefits of clean-air scenarios (e.g., reduction of carbon dioxide, black carbon, and methane) to achieve $PM_{2.5}$ and typographic ozone targets in delineated airsheds and pledge combined funding for climate change, AQM, and economic development, including improved health service. The step can be promoted in low-income emission regions.

Annex: Methodology

This research employs well-established scientific tools and methods to provide a holistic perspective on air quality in South Asia and to explore the costs and benefits of alternative policy intervention options to reduce air pollution in the region. As a starting point for subsequent strategic analyses, a comprehensive assessment of the state of air quality in South Asia reveals the sources of pollution and how they affect cities and regions.

Validated by available air quality monitoring data, the information emerges from calculations using the Greenhouse Gas–Air Pollution Interactions and Synergies (GAINS) model. It provides a holistic perspective on the chain of pollution. Starting from socioeconomic drivers, the model quantifies emissions and their dispersion in the atmosphere and estimates the multiple impacts on air quality and human health.

The model assesses the improvements offered by about 2,000 proven measures to reduce emissions, estimates their costs, and quantifies their side effects on greenhouse gas (GHG) emissions. The cost-effectiveness analysis of the GAINS model identifies packages of measures that deliver exogenously specified policy targets on air quality and/or GHG emissions at least cost.

Figure 35: Information Flow in the Greenhouse Gas–Air Pollution Interactions and Synergies Model

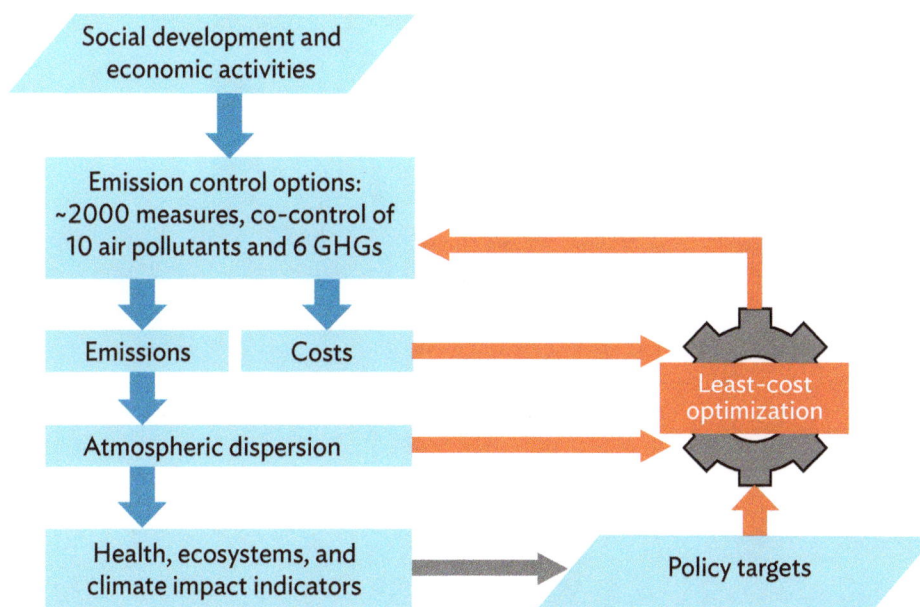

GAINS = Greenhouse Gas–Air Pollution Interactions and Synergies, IIASA = International Institute for Applied Systems Analysis, GHG = greenhouse gas.
Source: GAINS calculations, IIASA.

To capture the diversity across South Asia, the GAINS implementation for this flagship research distinguishes 31 emission source regions, i.e., states and provinces of large countries. The impacts of their emissions on regional air quality are computed for more than 500 cities, as well as for rural areas, with a spatial resolution of about 50 x 50 kilometers (0.5 x 0.5 degrees).

While air pollution has a wide range of negative impacts on human health (mortality and morbidity), agricultural crops, and natural ecosystems, this analysis focuses on the pollutant most harmful to human health: fine particulate matter ($PM_{2.5}$). The analysis does not assess additional threats to human health and vegetation caused by ground-level ozone, biodiversity threats from excess nitrogen deposition, and damage to sensitive terrestrial and aquatic ecosystems caused by acid deposition.

To tailor the findings to the diversity across South Asia, the research distinguishes 31 subregions. Any effective clean air strategy will vary in approach based on the context of each country or city, as well as its capacity to develop and implement measures. No uniform policy prescription for air quality applies to all countries and regions; it would neither be possible nor desirable for a problem that is so diverse in local circumstances.

The GAINS model considers the potential of about 400 different technical emission control measures, for which it estimates costs from a social planner's perspective. To explore the scope for cost-effective air quality improvements, the GAINS model considers about 400 end-of-pipe emission reduction measures for the various source categories, with their specific emission reduction efficiencies for all pollutants and GHGs, investments and operating costs, and application potentials.

The cost evaluation in GAINS quantifies the values to society of diverting resources to emission reduction. In practice, the values are approximated by estimating production costs rather than consumer prices. Therefore, any mark-ups charged over production costs by manufacturers or dealers do not represent actual resource use and are ignored. Any taxes added to production costs are similarly ignored as subsidies because they are transfers and not resource costs. Considering investments, operation and maintenance costs, and cost savings, total costs of specific measures are annualized over the full technical lifetime, applying a social interest rate of 4% to reflect the social planner's perspective of the GAINS analysis.

References

Bishop, K., J. Ketcham, and N. Kuminoff. 2018. Hazed and Confused: The Effect of Air Pollution on Dementia. *NBER Working Paper.* 24970. Cambridge, MA: National Bureau of Economic Research.

Bowe, B., Y. Xie, T. Li, Y. Yan, H. Xian, and Z. Ziyad Al-Aly. 2018. The 2016 Global and National Burden of Diabetes Mellitus Attributable to PM2·5 Air Pollution. *Lancet Planet Health.* 2. pp. 301–12.

Chang, T. Y., J. Graff Zivin, T. Gross, and M. Neidell. 2019. The Effect of Pollution on Worker Productivity: Evidence from Call Center Workers in China. *American Economic Journal: Applied Economics.* 11 (1). pp. 151–72.

Global Burden of Disease—Major Air Pollution Sources Working Group. 2018. Burden of Disease Attributable to Major Air Pollution Sources in India. *Special Report.* 21.

Lozano-Gracia, N. and M. Soppelsa. 2018. Pollution and City Competitiveness: A Descriptive Analysis, Draft Report. The World Bank, Washington, DC.

Murray, C. J., A. Y. Aravkin, P. Zheng, C. Abbafati, K. M. Abbas, M. Abbasi-Kangevari, ... and S. Borzouei. 2020. Global Burden of 87 Risk Factors in 204 Countries and Territories, 1990–2019: A Systematic Analysis for the Global Burden of Disease Study 2019. *The Lancet.* 396 (10258). pp. 1223–49.

Suades-González, E., M. Gascon, M. Guxens, and J. Sunyer. 2015. Air Pollution and Neuropsychological Development: A Review of the Latest Evidence. *Endocrinology.* 156 (10). pp. 3473–82.

World Bank. 2018. Pollution and City Competitiveness: A Descriptive Analysis, Draft Report, Lozano-Gracia, N. Soppelsa, M.E. The World Bank, Washington, DC.

———. 2020. *South Asia Economic Focus: Beaten or Broken?* Fall.

———. 2021. *The Global Health Cost of PM2.5 Air Pollution in 2019.* Washington, DC.

World Bank and Institute for Health Metrics and Evaluation. 2016. *The Cost of Air Pollution: Strengthening the Economic Case for Action.* Washington, DC.

6 Multilateral Development Banks as Key Partners in Promoting Regional Cooperation and Integration

Past and ongoing regional cooperation and integration efforts of multilateral development banks and the reach of their interventions tell a successful story. However, past successes do not always guarantee future successes under new circumstances.

Highlights

All economies in Asia and the Pacific have been affected by the coronavirus disease (COVID-19) crisis in many ways, but the impact is not uniform across countries and subregions. Virus containment measures have caused both demand- and supply-side shocks, and the knock-on effects have had enormous consequences for livelihoods.

As the world struggles, growing inequalities within and across countries and regions deserve our immediate attention. Poor and small enterprises are alarmingly more vulnerable to large-scale shocks, and pandemics exacerbate already-pressing inequality.

In such a fragile environment, interest is heightened in understanding what drives national and regional economic resilience. Already a hot topic since the 2009 global financial crisis, it is even more relevant today because of the scale and reach of COVID-19.

Substantial evidence in the literature and real-life case studies suggests that cooperation is a major determinant of economic resilience. Countries that cooperate with each other recover quickly from crises. Geographical proximity continues to play a major role in shaping global trade and investment trends as production fragmentation is concentrated among proximate trading partners, suggesting that regional cooperation and integration are key to boosting resilience in the long term.

The global consequences of the COVID-19 pandemic and its associated economic crisis require interregional cooperation among economic blocs. Multilateral development banks are well positioned to lay the ground for stronger interregional cooperation because of their experience, resources, and political leverage.

How Multilateral Development Banks Promote Regional Cooperation and Integration

Regional cooperation and integration (RCI) is complicated, requiring coordinated action at multiple levels, including public authorities, businesses, civil society organizations, and bilateral and multilateral cooperation agencies. An RCI policy has broad implications, including but not limited to international trade and investment flows, the governance of regional public goods, transnational social cohesion, and socioeconomic development in disadvantaged border regions (Börzel and Risse 2016). Therefore, the scope of supplementary RCI policies is broad, comprising physical infrastructure connectivity, harmonization of economic engagement procedures, the environment, and regional cohesion and identity building.

Multilateral Development Banks' Regional Cooperation and Integration Mandate and Strategies

Recognizing the need for multilateral cooperation on regional integration, multilateral development banks (MDBs) have traditionally and actively promoted RCI in their member countries. The Asian Development Bank (ADB) launched its first formal RCI policy in 1994 (ADB 2015), renewed it in 2006, and positioned itself as a financier, capacity builder, catalyst, and knowledge leader of RCI in Asia and the Pacific. ADB recently adopted the RCI Operational Plan (2019–2024) in line with its Strategy 2030 priorities. ADB's RCI activities rely on a large set of policy instruments, including massive subregional investment programs, RCI trust funds, and various capacity-building and knowledge-sharing initiatives. ADB is the secretariat for the Central Asia Regional Economic Cooperation (CAREC) Program, Greater Mekong Subregion, and South Asia Subregional Economic Cooperation (SASEC) Program, helping them identify and leverage RCI opportunities based on global, regional, and sector and thematic analyses.

The World Bank is managing holistic RCI programs in South Asia, sub-Saharan Africa, Middle East and North Africa, Central Asia, and East Asia and the Pacific. In South Asia, the World Bank marked the 10th anniversary of its regional program in 2020 and took the opportunity to update its South Asia Regional Integration, Cooperation and Engagement Approach (SA RICE for 2020–2023), which has three focus areas: (i) enabling economic connectivity, (ii) reducing vulnerabilities and building resilience, and (iii) investing in human capital, with an emphasis on gender across all activities. The focus on human capital has been recently added to the program in response to the pandemic. The International Development Association (IDA) Regional Window, launched in IDA13 as a pilot program, is one of the World Bank's main tools for supporting regional projects. It provides top-up funding for eligible regional investments and expedites collective action to meet shared goals, while taking advantage of economies of scale by encouraging countries to act together (World Bank 2019).

The European Bank for Reconstruction and Development (EBRD) has backed several large projects to integrate its countries of operation with European or Eurasian economic systems by financing physical infrastructure and supporting institutional and regulatory changes (soft integration measures). In mid-2017,

Recognizing the need for multilateral cooperation on regional integration, multilateral development banks have traditionally and actively promoted regional cooperation and integration in their member countries.

regional integration was formally introduced into EBRD's reshaped transition framework, which defines it as "increased interactions and strengthened links between economies" (EBRD 2020).

The Asian Infrastructure Investment Bank (AIIB) actively supports RCI projects that complement cross-border infrastructure connectivity by generating direct measurable benefits from strengthening regional trade, investment, and digital and financial integration across Asian economies and between Asia and the global economy. Connectivity and regional cooperation are one of four thematic priorities of AIIB, along with green infrastructure, technology-enabled infrastructure, and private sector mobilization (AIIB 2021).

Figure 36: Islamic Development Bank's Regional Cooperation and Integration Policy and Operational Strategy 2019

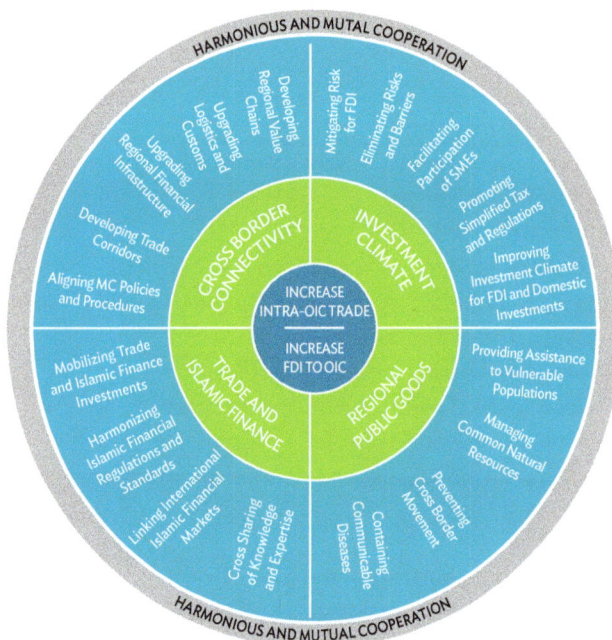

FDI = foreign direct investment, MC = member country, OIC = Organisation of Islamic Cooperation, SMEs = small and medium-sized enterprises.
Source: Islamic Development Bank.

The members of the Islamic Development Bank (IsDB) come only from the Global South: 57 countries spread across Asia, Africa, Europe, and South America. IsDB's core mandate is to expedite economic cooperation and integration among its member countries. IsDB has actively supported RCI activities since its inception and launched its first formal RCI Policy and Operational Strategy in 2019. The policy aims to enable IsDB to become a primary connecting platform for its members, regional cooperation organizations (RCOs), and communities to cooperate with each other. The policy is built on four pillars: (i) strengthening border connectivity, (ii) improving the investment climate and foreign direct investment, (iii) promoting Islamic trade and finance, and (iv) supporting regional public goods (IsDB 2019a). IsDB allocates a significant share (about 30%) of financing annually to regional projects.

Multilateral Development Bank Instruments to Support Regional Cooperation and Integration

MDBs use a wide array of instruments to support RCI. They include project and trade financing, trade facilitation, capacity building, triangular cooperation, as well as private sector operations, including investment and export credit guarantee schemes and public–private partnership arrangements.

An example of cross-border infrastructure project financing is IsDB's focus on transport and energy, which account for more than 70% of the bank's total regional infrastructure project approvals (IsDB 2019b). IsDB Group entities support RCI in compliance with their own mandates. The International Islamic Trade Finance Corporation has a global footprint in promoting trade and integration, particularly in energy, finance, and agriculture. The Islamic Corporation for the Insurance of Investment and Export Credit has a key role in building a conducive environment for RCI initiatives by providing safeguards to ease the expansion of investments and exports among IsDB member countries. The Islamic Corporation for the Development of the Private Sector helps promote RCI in IsDB member countries and subregions by financing cross-border private sector investments and improving investment ecosystems.

IsDB's RCI Department manages four main programs to advance the bank's regional integration agenda. The RCI Grant Program provides soft capacity support and technical assistance that complement IsDB's hard infrastructure interventions. Priority is given to capacity building to accelerate connecting landlocked IsDB member countries to international ports and maritime routes.

The Technical Assistance Program for Regional and Global Integration builds the institutional and human capacities of IsDB member countries to negotiate multilateral trade agreements, such as those discussed under the auspices of the World Trade Organization and others, to help countries participate in the global economy and to foster regional integration.

The Investment Promotion Technical Assistance Program aims to strengthen the capacity of IsDB member countries' investment promotion agencies and intermediaries to improve the investment climate and to attract domestic and foreign investment that contributes to sustainable development.

Finally, IsDB has a pioneering South–South cooperation mechanism—reverse linkage—which promotes RCI among IsDB member countries and beyond. Through the mechanism, IsDB identifies existing know-how, expertise, technology, and resources, and transfers them to those in need to achieve sustainable development outcomes. The mechanism is based on a peer-to-peer approach, which leads to strong ownership by the provider and by the recipient. The mechanism's bottom-up approach, involving all stakeholders, ensures that they all have a say in crafting solutions, which ensures sustainability. Reverse linkage has been successfully utilized in a diverse range of sectors and themes, and RCI is a priority, complementing IsDB's other capacity-building interventions.

Past and ongoing RCI efforts of MDBs and the reach of their interventions tell a successful story. However, past successes do not always guarantee future successes under new circumstances. The global governance system involves new actors, including RCOs, multinational corporations, and civil society organizations. They already form a complex landscape of global governance: plurilateral platforms (such as the G20), comprehensive bilateral agreements (particularly in trade), regional political organizations, and multi-actor coalitions focusing on specific issues (such as the environment) (Telo 2020). Accelerating RCI efforts, therefore, requires close coordination between many stakeholders, not only the public sector but also civil society and the private sector.

MDBs have been key in supporting RCI, particularly through intergovernmental regional integration schemes (Bull and Boas 2003). However, more efforts are needed to promote RCI from below in partnership with public policy actors, private businesses, academics, and civil society, while easing exchange of experience among peer countries. Utilizing new modalities of

South–South cooperation (e.g., IsDB's reverse linkage mechanism) and involving subnational actors (such as border-region localities) in RCI policy making are emerging issues in regional integration governance.

Recovering from the Pandemic

All economies in Asia have been affected by the COVID-19 crisis in many ways. The virus containment measures have caused both demand- and supply-side shocks, and the knock-on effects have had enormous consequences for livelihoods. The total gross domestic product (GDP) of emerging and developing Asia contracted by 1% but is expected to start recovering, with projected growth of 8.6% in 2021 (IMF 2021). The Organisation for Economic Co-operation and Development (2021), however, projects that global GDP growth will be only 5.5% in 2021 and that global output will rise above the pre-pandemic level by mid-2021.

If economic growth projections hold true, Asia will be on track to expedient recovery. But we should remember that macro projections are meaningful only when put into a larger developmental context considering social inclusiveness and sustainability. An ADB report predicts that disruption in economic activity because of the COVID-19 pandemic increased the extreme poverty rate in 35 developing Asian countries by about 2 percentage points in 2020, compared with a scenario without COVID-19 (Martinez and Bulan 2021). Growing inequalities within and between Asian economies constitute a critical risk to deepening integration by undermining potential gains, especially for economies that are catching up.

Role of Regional Cooperation Organizations, Regional Cooperation Platforms, and Multilateral Development Banks

Regional efforts to handle the crisis were neither a full success nor a total failure. The unprecedented nature of the crisis limited the possibility of drawing up a cohesive strategy to manage the pandemic response, especially at the beginning. Countries acted on their own with almost no coordination and harmonization even with their immediate neighbors (IsDB 2021). For example, uncoordinated border closures and unilateral travel bans complicated the handling of the crisis in many parts of the world.

Policy coordination–focused RCOs and operations-focused regional cooperation platforms, however, have been important in supporting recovery across Asia and the Pacific. They linked national and regional agendas and provided venues to expedite cooperation with development partners, which helped countries mobilize diverse advisory, technical, and financial support, including from MDBs.

The Association of Southeast Asian Nations, for example, activated pandemic preparedness protocols for travel and tourism, sharing of best practices, and strengthening of response capabilities. South Asian leaders established the COVID-19 Emergency Fund under the South Asian Association for Regional Cooperation. The Economic Cooperation Organization issued guidelines on cross-border facilitation measures to maintain regular supplies. All the efforts were timely. RCOs and regional cooperation platforms have proved that they are adept at designing innovative financing schemes and knowledge exchange platforms and at introducing common standards for the smooth functioning of trade and maintenance of supply chains across Asia.

MDBs implemented large-scale anti-crisis programs and provided countercyclical support to developing and least developed countries. For instance, at the beginning of the pandemic, IsDB approved the $2.3 billion Strategic Preparedness and Response Program (SPRP) to assist its member countries. The program takes a holistic approach: respond, restore, and restart. The three tracks are designed to help IsDB member countries recover from the impact of the COVID-19 pandemic by supporting health, economic, and social interventions.

Figure 37: Holistic 3-R Approach to Supporting Developing Countries during COVID-19

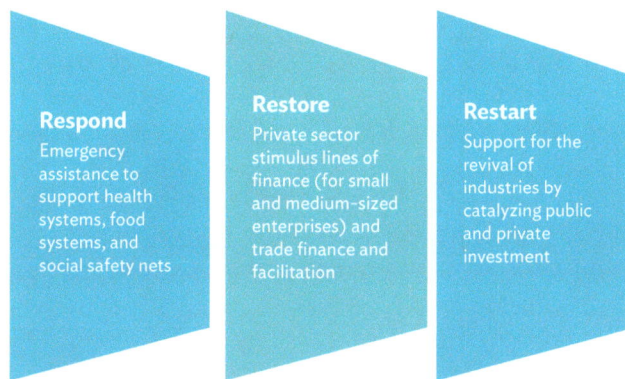

Respond
Emergency assistance to support health systems, food systems, and social safety nets

Restore
Private sector stimulus lines of finance (for small and medium-sized enterprises) and trade finance and facilitation

Restart
Support for the revival of industries by catalyzing public and private investment

COVID-19 = coronavirus disease.
Source: Islamic Development Bank.

IsDB estimated that 55 million people have benefited from IsDB's various COVID-19 response programs, including nearly 9 million who received food. The programs procured 5 million test kits and 9 million sets of personal protective equipment for health workers. The programs set up nearly 1,700 COVID-19 test centers and trained 20,000 health workers to better handle COVID-19 cases. The SPRP recognizes that activities to maintain basic livelihoods must be supported and, therefore, allocated 19% of its financing to support small and medium-sized enterprises (SMEs). IsDB helped provide social safety nets by supporting more than 10,000 SMEs, securing nearly 225,000jobs, and delivering finance to another 12,000 people (IsDB 2020a).

As part of the SPRP, IsDB has scaled up its reverse linkage interventions to support regional coordination during the pandemic. As a South–South cooperation modality, the mechanism had been used extensively to facilitate the transfer of

IsDB's experience with Islamic finance and South–South cooperation through the reverse linkage mechanism, ADB's successful subregional cooperation platforms, the World Bank's global reach, AIIB's strong focus on sustainable infrastructure, and EBRD's unique expertise in managing economic transition all reflect the strong complementarities of multilateral development banks.

knowledge and expertise between countries long before the pandemic. But the pandemic has witnessed the wide-scale use of the modality to connect countries with each other regionally. IsDB has initiated a reverse linkage program to build capacities of national medical laboratories in its member countries. The program benefits from peer learning to help participating countries coordinate their pandemic preparedness and response efforts regionally. A project between the Pasteur Institute of Dakar and a network of 10 laboratories in sub-Saharan Africa is being implemented. The program helps promote interregional cooperation, with the Government of the People's Republic of China cooperating with IsDB to help the least developed member countries of IsDB fight the pandemic.

Another example of reverse linkage, which complements the abovementioned program, is IsDB's electronic learning platform, launched to smooth peer learning between medical staff in Africa, who benefit from the expertise and experience of countries that are advanced in dealing with the pandemic in Africa and globally.

All other MDBs have launched massive pandemic response packages in a response greater than the response to the 2007–2008 global financial crisis. Their support has been extraordinary, particularly for the least-developed countries, achieved by front-loading concessional resources. For middle-income countries, MDBs' non-concessional lending windows provided access to long-term finance at below-market rates. MDBs had some flexibility for a short-term response to the pandemic as many were recently capitalized. However, in the medium and long term, their financial capacity and headroom constraints may hamper their ability to reach out to a wider constituency (UN 2021), suggesting that innovative financing tools, including blended models, are necessary to extend MDBs' reach.

To coordinate MDB efforts, the Heads of MDBs meetings are held regularly to exchange ideas and experiences. The first meeting in 2020 was chaired by IsDB. All MDBs reiterated their commitment to step up efforts to explore new avenues to provide low-cost financing for MDB members and scale up MDBs' collective response to COVID-19. Technical bilateral and multiparty engagements will complement the efforts. During the 2020 G20 Summit, a special discussion was dedicated to the COVID-19 pandemic and recommended additional actions to bolster MDBs' global efforts.

There is always room, however, for better cross-fertilization of MDBs' strengths, expertise, and experience. IsDB's experience with Islamic finance and South–South cooperation through the reverse linkage mechanism, ADB's successful subregional cooperation platforms such as the CAREC Program, the World Bank's global experience and reach, AIIB's strong focus on sustainable infrastructure, and EBRD's unique expertise in managing economic transition all reflect MDBs' strong complementarities, particularly in the post–COVID-19 era.

New avenues of cooperation should be opened with RCOs because they can bridge global and national policies. IsDB's experience in organizing consultative forums with RCOs in 2016, 2017, and 2019 is a good example. As already proven, RCOs and regional platforms can strengthen disease surveillance; mobilize supply chains; facilitate regional trade; and support the production and procurement of vaccines, medicines, and medical supplies through pooled purchasing to ensure lower prices and to equalize the negotiating power of lower-income countries (Amaya and De Lombaerde 2021). Such cooperation is particularly important in a post–COVID-19 world, where regional value chains are undergoing structural change as the pandemic has reinforced relocation and reshoring trends because of concerns about vulnerability to global shocks (Fortunato 2020).

Emerging Lessons: Digitalization and Innovative Financing Imperatives

Plenty of lessons may be learned from the crisis, which can guide RCI efforts across the globe. Digital trade was central in ensuring the smooth flow of essential goods across borders by reducing the need for physical contact during cross-border logistical operations and trade transactions. Some countries that had previously allowed only original paper documents now accept electronic customs declarations and other certificates, but the shift does require sufficient digital infrastructure, connectivity, legislative reforms, and skills (UNESCAP 2021). Now, there is an opportunity to convert these practices into long-term arrangements by scaling up the use of digital trade and payment systems under harmonized rules and procedures across Asia and the Pacific and beyond.

Digital technology opportunities are abundant, but they do not come without challenges. In Asia, only 26% of the rural population has access to broadband, and women are 10% less likely to own a mobile phone; the gap is 28% in South Asia (AIIB 2020). The digital divide is a major impediment to inclusive digital transformation. From an equity perspective, digital platforms are double-edged. While they offer access to many opportunities for small businesses, they benefit few because of strong network effects and economies of scale (ADB 2021). Without ignoring other RCI priorities, more resources must be invested in digital infrastructure connectivity and upgrading of digital skills to leverage the existing momentum of digital transformation in large segments of societies. Doing so will empower disadvantaged people to participate in digital transformation while helping small enterprises better integrate into larger markets.

More investment in digital technologies will equalize the playing field between developed and developing countries. As MDBs prioritize Asia's digital transformation in the post–COVID-19 era, they need to utilize innovative tools of financing. Islamic finance offers many opportunities to ensure inclusive access to financing services in the developing and developed worlds.

Various Islamic finance tools combine philanthropy and revenue generation and can expand access to financial services. The tools include *awqaf* (endowed trust funds), which, when embedded in social projects, can boost long-term resilience (IsDB 2021). Islamic finance can be a means of reaching out to communities across Asia to bolster MDB support's inclusiveness during and in the aftermath of COVID-19. Profit and loss sharing based on Islamic finance has huge potential to ease start-ups' access to capital in the age of digital transformation.

Islamic finance can be a critical source of development financing. In 2020, for example, IsDB raised $1.5 billion with its first-ever sustainability *sukuk* (Islamic bonds) to support its member countries in the aftermath of the COVID-19 pandemic. Proceeds from the debut issuance will be deployed exclusively for social projects under IsDB's Sustainable Finance Framework. The focus will be on access to essential services and SME financing and job creation in line with the Sustainable Development Goals. The *sukuk* can serve as a model for other financial institutions, corporate and sovereign, to help industries recover from the pandemic (IsDB 2020b).

The principles of Islamic finance help ward off endogenous crises such as the global financial crisis and provide a strong safety net against exogenous crises such as COVID-19. However, a spectrum of well-functioning institutions are required to translate these principles into tangible real-world impact. Inter-MDB and MDB–RCO cooperation can help the industry grow in harmony and pave the way for international agreements on regulatory and operational standards. Such cooperation will help countries and regions cope with the emerging challenges imposed by the COVID-19 crisis and strengthen their resilience to possible future shocks.

Key Messages and Policy Recommendations

- There is room for better cross-fertilization of MDBs' strengths and experience. IsDB's experience with Islamic finance and South–South cooperation through reverse linkage, ADB's successful subregional cooperation platforms such as the CAREC Program, the World Bank's global experience and reach, AIIB's strong focus on sustainable infrastructure, and EBRD's unique expertise in managing economic transition reflect MDBs' strong complementarities in the aftermath of COVID-19.

- MDBs and RCOs can bridge global and national policies to strengthen disease surveillance; improve national and global pandemic preparedness and response capacity; exchange experiences; and coordinate policies related to infrastructure connectivity, trade facilitation, and digital transformation.

- More efforts are needed to promote RCI from below by utilizing new modalities of South–South cooperation (e.g., IsDB's reverse linkage mechanism). The efforts include involving subnational actors in RCI policy making, forging closer cooperation between MDBs and RCOs to build shared regional integration visions, executing RCI programs, and promoting socioeconomic cohesion across borders with a focus on the vulnerable and disadvantaged.

- Health has been traditionally regarded as a domestic policy area (unlike trade, competition, intellectual property rights, or climate change). However, the COVID-19 pandemic has proved that health is a cross-border sector that requires not only multilevel and multi-actor cooperation but also global delivery of inclusive health-care services to maintain sustainable development.

- A regional public health policy cannot exist in isolation from other policy areas such as the regulation of movement of people, climate change, digital transformation and uptake, upgrading of skills, cooperation for data standardization, and international data sharing.

- The Asia and Pacific region is huge, with heterogenous socioeconomic characteristics, and can take an inter-subregional approach to accommodate differences.

- In the post–COVID-19 era, more resources must be invested in digital technologies to equalize the playing field between developed and developing countries.

- MDBs and RCOs need to align their priorities with the needs of the post–COVID-19 world. Innovative financing tools, including Islamic finance modalities and blended finance models, can be utilized to help countries and regions cope with the emerging challenges imposed by the pandemic.

References

Amaya, A. B. and P. de Lombaerde. 2021. Regional Cooperation is Essential to Combatting Health Emergencies in the Global South. *Globalization and Health.* 17 (1). pp. 1–6.

Asian Development Bank (ADB). 2015. *ADB Support to Regional Cooperation and Integration.* Manila.

ADB. 2021. *ADB Asian Economic Integration Report: Making Digital Platforms Work for Asia and the Pacific.* Manila.

Asian Infrastructure Investment Bank (AIIB). 2020. Investing to Address the Digital Divide in Asia. Beijing.

AIIB. 2021. AIIB Business Plan and Strategies: Strategic Programming. Beijing.

Börzel, T. A. and T. Risse (eds.). 2016. *The Oxford Handbook of Comparative Regionalism.* Oxford: Oxford University Press.

Bull, B. and M. Boas. 2003. Multilateral Development Banks as Regionalising Actors: The Asian Development Bank and the Inter-American Development Bank. *New Political Economy.* 8 (2). pp. 245–61.

European Bank for Reconstruction and Development (EBRD). 2020. *Cluster Evaluation: Projects Supporting Cross-Border Connectivity (Regional Integration).* London.

Fortunato, P. 2020. How COVID-19 is Changing Global Value Chains. United Nations Conference on Trade and Development. Geneva.

International Institute for Applied Systems Analysis (IIASA). The GAINS Model.

International Monetary Fund (IMF). 2021. *World Economic Outlook: Managing Divergent Recoveries.* Washington, DC.

Islamic Development Bank (IsDB). 2019a. *RCI Policy: Achieving Sustainable and Inter-Dependent Growth through Mutual Cooperation.* Jeddah.

IsDB. 2019b. *IsDB Regional Cooperation and Integration (RCI) Baseline Report.* Jeddah.

———. 2020a. *Development Effectiveness Report: Achieving Results during COVID-19 Pandemic.* Jeddah.

———. 2020b. *The COVID-19 Crisis and Islamic Finance: Response of the IsDB Group. Discussion draft.* Jeddah.

IsDB. 2021. *Impact of COVID-19 on Regional Cooperation and Integration (RCI) Thematic Areas.* Jeddah.

Martinez, A. and J. Bulan. 2021. We Are Just Now Discovering How Devastating COVID-19 Has Been for the Very Poor. *Asian Development Blog.* Manila.

Organisation for Economic Co-operation and Development (OECD). 2021. *OECD Economic Outlook Interim Report March 2021.* Paris.

Telo, M. (ed.). 2020. *Reforming Multilateralism in Post-COVID Times.* Brussels: Foundation for European Progressive Studies.

United Nations. 2021. *Financing for Sustainable Development Report 2021: Report of the Inter-Agency Task Force on Financing for Development.* New York.

United Nations Economic and Social Commission for Asia and the Pacific (UNESCAP). 2021. *Building Back Better from Crises through Regional Cooperation in Asia and the Pacific: Executive Summary.* Bangkok.

World Bank. 2019. *Two to Tango: An Evaluation of World Bank Group Support to Fostering Regional Integration.* Washington, DC.

CLOSING

The true value of any development publication is not related to its preparation, publication, or even its dissemination, but to its use. We constantly kept this principle in mind while cooperating and engaging with multilateral development bank (MDB) colleagues involved in creating the report. We believe it is usable and hope it *will* be used by the many regional cooperation and integration (RCI) practitioners across Asia and the Pacific.

The report provides insights on real-world examples of how countries, assisted by MDBs, turned quickly to wider and deeper RCI to face an unprecedented challenge that risked the welfare of every nation and person in the region. While countries and MDBs have some helpful experience responding to cross-border health challenges, the coronavirus disease (COVID-19) was on an entirely different level, and it demanded intercountry coordination and collaboration and MDB assistance on regional health security at a scale and intensity not seen before. And the pandemic demanded innovation, new ideas, new approaches. As the report demonstrates, to a great extent—although not entirely or perfectly or to the same extent everywhere simultaneously— countries led concerted, productive, and beneficial efforts to combat the pandemic. With valuable MDB assistance they have helped avert what could have been a much larger loss of life and material welfare. The report identifies crucial lessons for the reader's careful consideration.

The report provides other concrete examples of RCI and of MDB assistance that is striving to realize a region-wide transition from emergency to recovery and to put in place some initial foundations to build the recovery. The reader is urged to pay particular attention to the nature and degree of RCI innovation that is being attempted and reflected in those examples. What they show is that the region's RCI is also attempting to exploit—using new approaches—new cross-border opportunities that have emerged from the pandemic.

Several theme chapters take a medium- to longer-term perspective. In doing so, they have generated thought-provoking, research-based results to guide the formulation of country, regional, and interregional RCI policy and sector and thematic strategies in support of inclusive and sustainable recovery. Readers who are regional policy makers or sector and thematic planners or MDB officials charged with developing large RCI programs will likely find them timely and valuable.

Finally, the report points to what may be judged as the indispensable role and the efficacy of the established RCI subregional programs and other leading regional cooperation organizations such as the Pacific Community. This RCI architecture has been built and evolved by countries' own efforts and with indispensable and sustained support of MDBs. The pragmatic, flexible, consensus-based, and operational-focused nature and practices of the region's RCI architecture enabled countries and MDBs to act decisively against the pandemic. Those same characteristics will help support an RCI-based recovery. That said, the report also points to a growing need for the RCI architecture to encompass *a greater degree of inter-subregional cooperation*, congruent with the expanding spatial impacts of challenges and opportunities of climate change and digital trade, among other regional public goods. RCI practitioners must find ways to retain the strong sense of subregional solidarity that exists in the established RCI platforms while enabling the RCI architecture to meet head on enormous region-wide challenges.